MACMILLAN MASTER

General Editor: James Gibson
Published

JANE AUSTEN	*Emma* Norman Page
	Pride and Prejudice Raymond Wilson
	Mansfield Park Richard Wirdnam
ROBERT BOLT	*A Man for all Seasons* Leonard Smith
EMILY BRONTË	*Wuthering Heights* Hilda D. Spear
GEOFFREY CHAUCER	*The Miller's Tale* Michael Alexander
	The Prologue to the Canterbury Tales Nigel Thomas and Richard Swan
CHARLES DICKENS	*Bleak House* Dennis Butts
	Great Expectations Dennis Butts
	Hard Times Norman Page
GEORGE ELIOT	*Middlemarch* Graham Handley
	Silas Marner Graham Handley
	The Mill on the Floss Helen Wheeler
E.M. FORSTER	*A Passage to India* Hilda D. Spear
THE METAPHYSICAL POETS	Joan van Emden
WILLIAM GOLDING	*The Spire* Rosemary Sumner
	Lord of the Flies Raymond Wilson
OLIVER GOLDSMITH	*She Stoops to Conquer* Paul Ranger
THOMAS HARDY	*The Mayor of Casterbridge* Ray Evans
	Tess of the D'Urbervilles James Gibson
	Far from the Madding Crowd Colin Temblett-Wood
PHILIP LARKIN	*The Less Deceived and The Whitsun Wedding* Andrew Swarbrick
D.H. LAWRENCE	*Sons and Lovers* Ronald Draper
CHRISTOPHER MARLOWE	*Doctor Faustus* David A. Male
THOMAS MIDDLETON and WILLIAM ROWLEY	*The Changeling* Tony Bromham
ARTHUR MILLER	*The Crucible* Leonard Smith
GEORGE ORWELL	*Animal Farm* Jean Armstrong
WILLIAM SHAKESPEARE	*Hamlet* Jean Brooks
	King Lear Francis Casey
	The Winter's Tale Diana Devlin
	Julius Caesar David Elloway
	Macbeth David Elloway
	Measure for Measure Mark Lilly
	A Midsummer Night's Dream Kenneth Pickering

MACMILLAN MASTER GUIDES

	Henry IV Part I Helen Morris
	Romeo and Juliet Helen Morris
	The Tempest Kenneth Pickering
GEORGE BERNARD SHAW	*St Joan* Leonée Ormond
RICHARD SHERIDAN	*The School for Scandal* Paul Ranger
	The Rivals Jeremy Rowe
JOHN WEBSTER	*The White Devil and The Duchess of Malfi* David A. Male

Forthcoming

JANE AUSTEN	*Sense and Sensibility* Judy Simons
SAMUEL BECKETT	*Waiting for Godot* Jennifer Birkett
WILLIAM BLAKE	*Songs of Innocence and Songs of Experience* Alan Tomlinson
GEOFFREY CHAUCER	*The Pardoner's Tale* Geoff Lester
	The Wife of Bath's Tale Nicholas Marsh
	The Knight's Tale Anne Samson
T.S. ELIOT	*Murder in the Cathedral* Paul Lapworth
HENRY FIELDING	*Joseph Andrews* Trevor Johnson
E.M. FORSTER	*Howard's End* Ian Milligan
GERARD MANLEY HOPKINS	*Selected Poems* R. Watt
BEN JONSON	*Volpone* Michael Stout
JOHN KEATS	*Selected Poems* John Garrett
HARPER LEE	*To Kill a Mockingbird* Jean Armstrong
ARTHUR MILLER	*Death of a Salesman* Peter Spalding
WILLIAM SHAKESPEARE	*Richard II* Charles Barber
	Othello Christopher Beddowes
	Henry V Peter Davison
	As You Like It Kiernan Ryan
	Twelfth Night Edward Leeson
ALFRED TENNYSON	*In Memoriam* Richard Gill

Further titles are in preparation

MACMILLAN MASTER GUIDES
THE WHITE DEVIL AND
THE DUCHESS OF MALFI
BY JOHN WEBSTER

DAVID A. MALE

MACMILLAN

First edition 1986

Published by
MACMILLAN EDUCATION LTD
Houndmills, Basingstoke, Hampshire RG21 2XS
and London
Companies and representatives
throughout the world

Typeset in Great Britain by
TEC SET, Sutton, Surrey

Printed in Hong Kong

British Library Cataloguing in Publication Data
Male, David A.
The white devil and The Duchess of Malfi by John
Webster. —(Macmillan master guides)
1. Webster, John, *1580? - 1625?* Duchess of Malfi
2. Webster, John, *1580? - 1625?* White devil
I. Title
822'.3   PR3184.D83
ISBN 0-333-40264-2 Pbk
ISBN 0-333-40377-0 Pbk export

CONTENTS

GENERAL EDITOR'S PREFACE

The aim of the Macmillan Master Guides is to help you to appreciate the book you are studying by providing information about it and by suggesting ways of reading and thinking about it which will lead to a fuller understanding. The section on the writer's life and background has been designed to illustrate those aspects of the writer's life which have influenced the work, and to place it in its personal and literary context. The summaries and critical commentary are of special importance in that each brief summary of the action is followed by an examination of the significant critical points. The space which might have been given to repetitive explanatory notes has been devoted to a detailed analysis of the kind of passage which might confront you in an examination. Literary criticism is concerned with both the broader aspects of the work being studied and with its detail. The ideas which meet us in reading a great work of literature, and their relevance to us today, are an essential part of our study, and our Guides look at the thought of their subject in some detail. But just as essential is the craft with which the writer has constructed his work of art, and this may be considered under several technical headings – characterisation, language, style and stagecraft, for example.

The authors of these Guides are all teachers and writers of wide experience, and they have chosen to write about books they admire and know well in the belief that they can communicate their admiration to you. But you yourself must read and know intimately the book you are studying. No one can do that for you. You should see this book as a lamppost. Use it to shed light, not to lean against. If you know your text and know what it is saying about life, and how it says it, then you will enjoy it, and there is no better way of passing an examination in literature.

JAMES GIBSON

GENERAL INTRODUCTION

Shakespeare's *A Midsummer Night's Dream* includes a scene in which some workmen, unskilled at acting, rehearse a play. One of them, Flute, a bellows-mender by trade, has been allotted the female role. He is very uncertain as to what is required of him. When he finally appears on the stage during a rehearsal he blurts out all that he has so painfully learnt. But the producer immediately reprimands him with the words: 'You speak all your part at once, cues and all'. Flute had learnt all the words and recited them in one continuous speech. There was nothing in his script to suggest that this was not the right action. His error is easily explained. The Elizabethan actor did not have the whole of the play written out, but only the words of his own speeches with a few lines from the previous speaker as cues to warn him when to begin. Only the producer's copy of the play would contain instructions for entrances and exits.

We must be careful not to fall into a similar trap when we read the text of a play by assuming that the words printed on the page *are* the play. Indeed they are not. We must recognise that the script of a play is very different from the text of a novel or a poem and requires quite different responses from us as readers. Perhaps the text of a play may best be considered as a printed set of instructions given to a company of actors in the hope that they will be translated into action on the stage in such a way that they still represent the author's original intention. Playwrights depend on actors as their agents of communication.

The dialogue of a play carries an immense burden. Not only does it convey the actual meaning of the play in terms of what the author intends to say but, apart from stage instructions, also provides information to the actor from which he draws many deductions and implications to be revealed in his characterisation. The actor must, in addition, pay attention to the sound and pattern of the vocalised words, uttering them in a manner appropriate to the personality, attitude and mood of the character. The literary style in which the play is written may sometimes be grand flowing poetic language, at others, very ordinary, everyday, colloquial. But it must still fit the character.

As well as the words of the text, the playwright will give 'stage instructions', indicating the kind of actions, movements or stage effects he requires. These instructions need very careful interpretation by the actors. We will find that John Webster is particularly interested in spectacular stage effects. He includes dumb shows for which only the briefest instructions are given. These little scenes are acted out in silent mime. For example, the Duchess of Malfi is forced to view a tableau of wax figures representing her dead husband and children. She supposes the bodies to be real. *The White Devil* includes a moving tableau depicting the gymnasium in which one of the characters has his neck broken at a vaulting horse. Many woundings and assassinations require very careful organisation and timing to be dramatically effective. Added to these are appearances of dancing, chanting madmen, mysterious ghosts and ghostly voices whose impact depends on the visual effect that they create. The words printed in the text are given life and meaning in performance. On the page these words look so inanimate, but when acted may induce hushed silence or hearty laughter from the audience. This strange power is derived partly from the meaning and emotion that the words contain, but also from their sound, the accents in which they are spoken, the careful use of pauses, timing and emphasis. When these vocal effects are combined with visual effects then the full impact of the text is finally experienced. As John Styan writes in *The Dramatic Experience* (Cambridge University Press, 1965, p.53) 'It is not the words alone which make the play, but the vivid dramatic impressions which the words can create'. When reading a play, we must be constantly on the alert, responsive to those impressions that build in our imagination a picture of dramatic reality.

In summary we may say that the words of a dramatic text have the following functions:

1. they create the literary or poetic style of the play;
2. they provide details from which characterisation can be developed;
3. they carry the plot of the play and its dramatic structure through a series of episodes animated by language in action;
4. they suggest the environment of the action and evoke particular moods or feelings.

When the text moves into actual production, the demands are further extended so that the words also:

5. provide ideas for staging the play;
6. offer suggestions to designers for settings and costumes.

ACKNOWLEDGEMENTS

Quotations are taken from *The Revels Plays* editions of Webster's plays: John Russell Brown (ed.) *The White Devil* (Manchester University Press, 1977); *The Duchess of Malfi* (Manchester University Press, 1976).

Cover illustration: *A Vanitas Still Life* by Pieter Claesz (c. 1590–1661). © Johnny Van Haeften Ltd, London, courtesy of the Bridgeman Art Library.

1 JOHN WEBSTER:
LIFE AND BACKGROUND

John Webster was very much a city man. He was born, educated, practised law and wrote his plays in the heart of London. This contact with life and work in the capital is reflected in his dramatic writings – but not directly. Webster's particular power was drawn from his careful and wide reading and his sharp observations of life as it was lived around him. His law studies brought inevitable contact with the legal world of judges and lawyers, court officials and parliament. The background of his life in London together with his avid reading supplied a continuous source of inspiration. These experiences were subtly absorbed into his plays, so as to present a fresh, individual mode of dramatic writing. Neither of his two greatest plays, *The White Devil* or *The Duchess of Malfi* was sited in England. Though lavish and full of Italianate bravado and excess, they nevertheless remained close to London in terms of their comment on the current social, political and moral issues and in their theatrical style. The literary sources might be European letters, novels and essays, but inspiration for the plays was derived from Webster's life in London. Every stage of his career contributed to his work as a playwright.

Webster's father was a wealthy coach-merchant who built and hired out coaches in London. His flourishing business, close by the City wall and near to the Law Courts, served the nearby fashionable houses and was convenient for Smithfield market where the trade was principally in horses. It was a bustling, thriving, bargaining world of law, nobility, commerce, with its private scandals and sensations mingling with the ceremony and dignity of court and parliament. Also in the vicinity of the Webster house were a number of theatres including the Fortune and The Red Bull. John Webster experienced life in a great city where thrusting energy, contention and a delight in entertainment combined to make it a world of colour, diversity and danger, not only from the lurking sneak-thieves and ne'er-do-wells who haunted Smithfield's Bartholomew's Fair but also from the ever-threatening plague.

Born about 1580, John Webster began his education at the Merchant Taylors' School which had come into prominence because of the advanced educational theories of its first headmaster, Richard Mulcaster. He believed in a broadly-based curriculum so that pupils received training not only in the classic subjects of Greek and Latin but also in the English language and literature for which Mulcaster had a special admiration. The boys also learnt music, engaged in a variety of physical activities (even football) and had experience of drama through theatrical performances. We do know that at one time the school's acting company was commanded to perform before the Queen at Hampton Court. So Webster's school-days gave him a taste for literature, a care for language, acquaintance with dramatic texts, and an introduction to the world of the theatre.

In 1598, he began to study law, being admitted into the Middle Temple, one of the law-training establishments in the Inns of Court. As well as being a teaching institution the Middle Temple also housed practising lawyers and barristers. In addition to concern for the law and legal procedures, there was a strong tradition of entertainment and celebrations ranging from the formal to the light-hearted. Records cite productions of classical or contemporary plays (for example, Shakespeare's *Twelfth Night* in 1602), masques and ceremonial processions as well as lively dancing and disguisings during the Christmas festivities. Some Middle Temple students gifted in composing verse or music supplied the texts, noted for their sharp wit, daring, even scurrility, in parodies, songs, mocking jests and comic orations. One of these students was John Marston who was to have a great influence on the young John Webster. We know little of his legal career, but studies in the Middle Temple certainly gave him a taste for the theatre. Attendance at ceremonies, celebrations, masques and festivities provided a rich feast of poetry, parody, oration and jest accompanied by solemn music or festive dancing. Exposure to court room trials, accusations, lawyers' verbal dexterity and judicial rulings also contributed to Webster's writing (for example, the trial in *The White Devil*). The city, nobility and officers of law and government gave Webster the experience of living in a sophisticated worldly, rich, City society: precisely the world of *The White Devil* and *The Duchess of Malfi*.

Webster must have been a voracious reader and, like many authors, he probably kept a commonplace book, that is, a note book in which he copied out sentences, sayings, maxims, attractive poetic couplets and numerous other literary quotations that took his fancy. All the commentators remark on his appetite for other men's writings. These are described as 'borrowings' rather than thefts, because Webster nearly always modified the quotations in such a way as to give their original flavour a different taste which marked his own inventiveness.

His contacts and experience in the City, particularly the theatrical activities, brought him into association with the nearby London theatres and acting companies that from time to time performed in the Inns of Court. The first records of his playwriting show him as a collaborator with other authors in producing the stream of plays necessary to meet the demands of the theatre. This collaborative method of playwriting was not unusual during this period. It was the means by which Webster learnt the craft of playwriting and what worked practically in the theatre. In his own preface to *The White Devil* (published in 1612) Webster recorded his debt to a number of contemporary authors – George Chapman, Ben Jonson, Francis Beaumont, John Fletcher, William Shakespeare, Thomas Dekker and John Heywood. The first payments to him for playwriting were in association with other writers. Philip Henslowe, who managed two important theatre companies, mentioned in his day-book a payment to John Webster, Anthony Munday, Michael Drayton and Thomas Middleton for their play *Caesar's Fall* and the diary went on to record several payments to groups of authors including Webster for playscripts. With Dekker, Webster wrote *Westward Ho* and *Northward Ho*. His journeyman plays were joint efforts that elaborated, extended or amended versions of other men's plays. They were not painfully constructed solitary products following an individualistic style. Such diverse literary, dramatic and theatrical experience shaped Webster's course as a playwright. It would be foolish to expect his plays not to reflect and exemplify that experience.

Webster's reputation rests principally on two plays – *The White Devil* and *The Duchess of Malfi*. The first was performed by the acting company known as The Queen's Men at the Red Bull Theatre in Clerkenwell. This theatre was in the neighbourhood of the Webster coach-yard. By the author's own account the premiere was not very successful. The theatre was open to the wintry air and the audience unresponsive, though the company's performance received Webster's approval. His next play was produced by a rival company – The King's Men. *The Duchess of Malfi* was effectively performed at the totally indoor Blackfriars Theatre in the City before a welcoming, sophisticated audience. Further performances took place at the Globe Theatre, a large public playhouse on the south bank of the river Thames. We look in vain for a sequel to this successful, much praised production which acquired three commendatory poems in its published version. The play was described as a masterpiece and Webster a poet whom neither Greece nor Rome could better. Later works – *The Devil's Law Case*, a descriptive poem of the Lord Mayor's Show, further collaborations and a final play *Appius and Virginia* (1623) – did not sustain the vigorous, imaginative thrust of the two major plays. The date of Webster's death is uncertain. It could have been as early as 1625 when he would have been 43 years old or as late as 1634.

Webster's genius as a playwright is represented most comprehensively by his two major plays. Though both were set in Italy, their structure and style reflected the sophisticated English drama of the early seventeenth century. Their subject matter found powerful contemporary parallels in the life of the court and the city of London. They combined his unique experience of London life and the lively competitive world of the theatre which he embraced with enthusiasm and skill as a collaborator, editor, commentator, poet and playwright.

PART I: THE WHITE DEVIL
2 SUMMARIES AND
CRITICAL COMMENTARY

Act I, Scene i

Summary

A street in Rome Count Lodovico has been banished from Rome for sundry misdoings and murders. Whilst reciting the various misdeeds, his comrades promise to seek his reinstatement. Lodovico is angry that Vittoria Corombona, a lady of Venice, has not supported his cause. (He takes to piracy but later returns to Padua.)

Commentary

The opening scene introduces Lodovico, a nobleman whose crimes, as his companions remind him, have properly led to his banishment. But he is quick to point out that other noblemen, like Bracciano, have committed greater crimes, yet they have gone unpunished. Vittoria has not helped him. We cannot condone his attitude, but recognise the uneven application of justice. Indeed the whole conversation between Lodovico and his companions exposes a very low opinion of integrity and justice in the world. Although he is not a major figure in the play, Lodovico acts as a connecting strand. His actions involve all the principal characters. As a disgruntled victim at odds with authority, Lodovico is an obvious candidate to participate in plans for revenge or acts of treachery against his opponents.

Act I, Scene ii

Summary

Camillo's House in Florence Flamineo, secretary to Bracciano and brother-in-law to Camillo, claims to have arranged a secret rendezvous between his sister Vittoria and his master. Both men are scornful of

Camillo, Vittoria's husband. Bracciano withdraws when Camillo enters. Camillo is suspicious of Bracciano, and admits a coolness in the relationship with his wife. Flamineo first advises Camillo to lock up Vittoria, but then argues that such a procedure would only ensure her determination to escape. Next, to avoid charges of jealousy, he suggests that absence of restraint might be the best method. In offering this advice, Flamineo pretends to seek a reconciliation between Vittoria and her husband, but in reality he is forwarding Bracciano's suit. Finally he urges Camillo to assume a distant and offhand attitude by locking himself in his bedroom. Camillo agrees and entrusts Flamineo with the key.

Bracciano re-enters the room to meet Vittoria, but their loving exchanges are overheard by Vittoria's mother, Cornelia. Vittoria recounts a dream in which her husband, Camillo, and Bracciano's wife, Isabella, accuse her of wanting to replace a well-grown yew with a withered blackthorn and then attempt to bury her alive. A whirlwind breaks a limb from the yew, striking the assailants dead. Bracciano asserts his protection, but at this point Cornelia interrupts to denounce the couple. She also reveals that Isabella has returned from Rome. After Vittoria and Bracciano leave, Flamineo upbraids his mother, saying he is willing to risk anything to improve his position since his family have left him so poorly provided for. Alone, Flamineo considers subtle ways by which he may pursue his own ends.

Commentary

This scene is crammed with incidents that set the complicated plot into quick action. Webster is more concerned with the outcome of events rather than the laborious establishment of relationships. Bracciano rapidly reveals his desire for Vittoria and her response is equally fast. We speedily identify Flamineo's readiness to act as pander to his sister and his gross views of sexual relationships and marriage are displayed in his crude language. He sees in Bracciano the opportunity for advancement and he is willing to deceive Camillo, plot with Vittoria and reject his mother's reprimands. Flamineo personifies the ambitious courtier ready to use any deviousness or duplicity to aid his personal aspirations. An added intensity is given to this manipulation because the participants are not distant strangers, but close family relatives among whom some kind of loyalty might be expected.

We also see in Vittoria's dream, the unusual method by which Webster advances the plot. The images prepare us for the actual dangers that are in store for Isabella and Camillo. Nightmare vision will become harsh reality. The opening of the scene includes Flamineo's crude observations, principally expressed in prose. The private exchanges between Bracciano and

Vittoria are couched in forceful verse that gives colour, vigour and speed in the closing sequence, heightening the excitement and hastening the pace.

Act II, Scene i

Summary

A room in Francisco's palace in Florence Francisco, Duke of Florence, greets his newly-returned sister Isabella. His secretary, Marcello (who is also brother to Vittoria), announces the arrival of Bracciano. Cardinal Monticelso is present and the two nobles reprimand Bracciano for his untoward behaviour with Vittoria, but the accusations are abruptly rejected. Francisco also complains that his messages to Bracciano concerning some troublesome pirates have gone unheeded. The Cardinal hopes that the breach between Bracciano and his wife will be healed by their son, Giovanni. But when Isabella returns, a fierce battle of words takes place between husband and wife. He alleges that she has been visiting a lover in Rome. Despite her denial, Bracciano vows never to sleep with her again. To avoid public scandal, Isabella urges that the vow should emanate from her so that Bracciano will not be blamed by the Duke. Then Isabella turns her venom on Vittoria for seducing Bracciano and, making a public announcement of her separation from her husband, departs for Padua.

Bracciano and Flamineo plot Isabella's death with Doctor Julio. Flamineo has already arranged the despatch of Camillo. The unfortunate man has received an emblem depicting a stag without horns which Cardinal Monticelso interprets as implying that Camillo has been cuckolded. Monticelso promises to supervise Vittoria's behaviour when he sends Camillo and Marcello to deal with the pirate attacks, but, in fact, it is simply a ruse to trap Bracciano since the chief pirate, Lodovico, has already moved to Padua (I.i.).

Commentary

This scene introduces the two other important characters in the play: Francisco, Duke of Florence, brother to Isabella, and Cardinal Monticelso. They represent political and religious power and are fiercely critical of any misdemeanour particularly when it affects family and morality. Though Francisco and Monticelso are assertive, selfish men, confident of their power, and antagonistic toward any who challenge their supremacy, they fail to intimidate Bracciano. The young Giovanni, son of Bracciano and Isabella, supplies the wit and naivety of youth. His jokes reduce the tension. The second section of the scene demonstrates the animosity between Bracciano and Isabella. He is suspicious of her expedition to

Rome and resents the pressures applied by Francisco. Clearly their marriage has broken down.

During the plotting of Camillo's murder, we notice that Flamineo's conversation with the doctor is full of unpleasant images - lechery, poisoning and bloodshed. The doctor's alleged healing skills are diminished to devices of murder. The emblem of the horns, like Vittoria's dream, informs us about character. It emphasises Camillo's failure as a husband as well as his cuckoldry. The apparent moralistic attitude of Monticelso and Francisco is shown to be spurious when the reason for Camillo's military posting is revealed. They hope that his absence will tempt Bracciano into further misconduct and thus precipitate his downfall. Lodovico is reintroduced to become an instrument in their plans for revenge.

Act II, Scene ii

Summary

A room in Camillo's house A conjuror produces two dumb shows for Bracciano. The first illustrates the poisoning of Isabella who, as a nightly habit, kisses the portrait of her husband. The lips on the canvas have been smeared with poison. A second dumb show portrays the murder of Camillo in the gymnasium. He is trapped at the vaulting horse by Flamineo and his neck broken. Flamineo and his brother (though Marcello was absent during the actual murder) are both arrested by the Cardinal and the Duke who soon appear on the scene. Because of the brothers' closeness to Vittoria, she is also suspected as an accomplice and plans are made for her apprehension.

Commentary

This scene, with its two contrasted dumb shows, one dark and mysterious, the other lively and action-packed, illustrates a non-realistic mode of presentation that gives Webster's play a particularly theatrical quality. The audience is intrigued by the conjuror with his denigration of third-rate exponents of the art and the superiority of his proposed magic demonstration. We are already aware of the dangers to Isabella and Camillo and these threats become reality through the highly artifical convention of the dumb shows. Normally these shows were used to introduce, in a stylised way, events that would subsequently become major elements in the main plot, but here they are used to accomplish the actual murders. Isabella and Camillo are now dead. In addition, in the first episode, Lodovico's devotion for Isabella becomes general knowledge. By placing these shows in close proximity with all that they reveal, the action of the play moves swiftly forward to Vittoria's arraignment, since it is suggested, with little obvious evidence, that she is directly implicated. Although the audience witnesses only magic shows, the effect is to compress complex events into a short, totally explicable, fast-moving, significant development of the main plot.

The scene also illustrates the machiavellian deceit that Bracciano and his agents employ to secure their own ends. The knowledge of Isabella's habit of kissing her husband's picture is used to destroy her. The virtuous Marcello is decoyed from the gymnasium in case he objects to the method by which Camillo is killed. Bracciano seems indifferent to the capture of his secretary and the innocent Marcello. He believes he can escape with Vittoria before the arresting officers arrive.

Act III, Scene i

Summary

The antechamber of Monticelso's mansion Francisco and Monticelso, by inviting the resident ambassadors to be present at Vittoria's trial, hope to destroy her reputation – though they realise the evidence is circumstantial. Flamineo jokes with the lawyers and ambassadors as they assemble, believing he is safe with the support of Bracciano. When Marcello reprimands him for his role as pander, Flamineo is unrepentant, chastising his brother for losing opportunities for advancement, secured, if necessary, by illegal action.

Commentary

The unscrupulous motives of the Cardinal and the Duke are exposed in this episode. The evidence is slight but the possibility of damaging publicity is substantial. We also see the strong contrast between the two brothers. The guilty, ambitious Flamineo is boastful, assured, confident of his employer's support and contemptuously ridicules the ambassadors. On the other hand, Marcello, whom we know to be innocent, is distressed by events that have darkened the family name. Flamineo's scurrilous sexual innuendoes in his chatter with the lawyers shows a complete lack of moral concern for his sister, whilst Marcello would rather see Vittoria dead than debauched.

Act III, Scene ii

Summary

A hall of Monticelso's mansion The arraignment of Vittoria. Unexpectedly Bracciano arrives for Vittoria's trial and is allowed to remain. When the lawyer commences the charges against Vittoria in Latin, she demands to be heard in Italian. But the official continues to speak in exaggerated legalese, and is dismissed by an annoyed Francisco. The Cardinal takes over the prosecution, beginning with a long denunciation of whores and suggesting that Vittoria is one. She is also accused of adultery and the murder of her husband. Her failure to wear mourning-clothes is cited as proof of her brazen attitude. In reply, Vittoria denies guilt, asserting that no real proof of her complicity has been offered. Monticelso interrupts, enquiring who was present at her house on the night of the murder. At this point, Bracciano intervenes. He admits his presence, but only as an adviser to Camillo concerning his debts to Monticelso. Following an angry exchange, Bracciano stalks out. Then the Cardinal produces a letter in which Bracciano proposes a secret rendezvous with Vittoria, enclosing a large sum of money. Vittoria denies that she agreed to any proposals in the letter and asserts that the money was to relieve Camillo's debts. She attacks the Cardinal for being both prosecutor and judge. He retorts that her conduct has always been notorious and she is sentenced to confinement in a house of convertites (penitential whores). Vittoria denounces the injustice of the punishment before she is taken away by guards. Both Flamineo and Marcello are released from their confinement.

After the trial, Bracciano reappears to seek reconciliation with Francisco. Flamineo, to avoid awkward questions, decides to adopt the pose of a madman – his insanity caused by the news of his sister's disgrace. Then the young Giovanni, dressed in black, announces the death of his mother, Isabella. To the distress of Duke Francisco the boy treats the matter very light-heartedly.

Commentary

This episode is striking for the skill by which the author gains our sympathy for Vittoria, although her liaison with Bracciano is well known, as is his complicity in the murder of Camillo. The trial is conducted in such a way as to present Vittoria as a victim rather than a guilty adultress. Throughout the scene her bravery in the face of hostility is notable. She stays calm before the whirlwind attack from the Cardinal – a speech demonstrating Webster's vivid rhetorical verse built round the reiterated question, 'What are whores?' Bracciano stays silent until Vittoria is charged with murdering her husband – an accusation which she adamantly denies. Having turned his intervention on her behalf into a threat of violence against Monticelso, he storms out leaving Vittoria even more isolated. She is very wary of Francisco's apparently milder words, boldly refuting the evidence of the letter, 'temptation to lust proves not the act'. Vittoria fearlessly challenges Monticelso as both judge and prosecutor. Finally, when the murderous Flamineo and his brother are pardoned (stressing the injustice of the whole proceedings), she curses her judges, defiantly exclaiming at her departure, 'through darkness diamonds spread their richest light'. With the English ambassador as a sympathetic spokesman, Webster skilfully invokes admiration for Vittoria's spirited defence though she is no innocent victim. We are unimpressed by the fierce denunciations of her accusers who as the critic L. Salingar points out are 'at once upholders of public convention and deep-dyed machiavellians'. They are, in other words, men, outwardly moralistic, but ready to adopt any devious unscrupulous means to achieve their own ends. The brief episode after the trial serves to develop Flamineo's devious scheming and also gives us a taste of the sharpness of young Giovanni's judgement which will be reiterated later in the play. The language and style of the whole court-proceedings reflect Webster's own experience in the lawcourts of London. The mocking portrait of the first prosecuting counsel has a strong sense of realism about it. Perhaps Webster had often heard such long-winded, convoluted speeches couched in incomprehensible Latin.

Act III, Scene iii

Summary

The antechamber of Monticelso's mansion Flamineo begins to act distractedly, refusing comfort from the ambassadors. Lodovico, who has now joined the courtiers, is suspicious of Flamineo's behaviour, knowing that the young man had been acting as pander between his sister and Bracciano. The two engage in teasing exchanges, each testing the other out. Flamineo is angered by the news that Lodovico has received a pension from Isabella and has attached himself to the court of the young prince.

Antonio and Gasparo, friends of Lodovico, bring news of the Pope's imminent death and the success of Francisco in obtaining a pardon for Lodovico. Delighted by his new prospects, the confident Lodovico now provokingly asserts that Vittoria is a whore and that Flamineo is the pander. A scuffle breaks out. Lodovico soon realises the depth of the animosity between himself and Vittoria's brothers.

Commentary

Flamineo's position has become somewhat hazardous as Act III closes. Vittoria has been condemned, Bracciano apparently reconciled with opponents and the exiled Lodovico has returned as companion to young Giovanni and is pardoned for his previous errors. By feigning madness, Flamineo hopes to avoid uncomfortable questions and protect his position. Following the pardon, Lodovico's temporary and uncertain friendship is quickly set aside. The need for Flamineo's influence has become superfluous.

Act IV, Scene i

Summary

Monticelso's mansion Though angry, Francisco is reluctant to seek revenge for his sister's poisoning. Cardinal Monticelso urges deception and produces a book which lists villains willing to undertake any treacherous work. Left alone to peruse the book, Francisco realises the extent of corruption in the city. In planning his revenge, he calls to mind his dead sister and the ghost of Isabella appears before him. He decides to write a feigned letter to Vittoria, now confined in the house of convertites. To incite Bracciano's jealousy, he ensures that the letter is delivered at a time when Bracciano's servant may see it. The newly-pardoned Lodovico is to be the instrument of revenge.

Commentary

This scene removes any ambiguity concerning the unscrupulousness and deceit of both Francisco and Monticelso. The Duke's desire to revenge his sister's death is fuelled by the Cardinal's provision of the list of knaves. The unacceptable face of politics and religion is laid bare. Any objective may be achieved through knavery, deceit or murder. The black book describes specialist agents for each type of misdeed.

The harsh reality of this encounter changes with the appearance of Isabella's ghost, conjured by the power of Francisco's melancholy. Webster causes vivid imagination to bring forth a spectre. First dream, then dumb show and now a ghost demonstrate the inner working of the mind.

The conversation between Francisco and Monticelso offers a powerful and ironic indictment of sharp practice and injustice. Crimes such as rape, murder, theft and treason are not to be remedied by the rule of law but by strategems and deceits. Vivid animal allegories – of the sleeping lion waiting to pounce, or the entrapping spider's web – suggest the methods. Descriptions of such wholesale deception may well owe more to Webster's knowledge of the city of London than to reports from distant Florence.

Act IV, Scene ii

Summary

The house of convertites Flamineo intercepts the letter delivered by Francisco's servant to Vittoria. Then it is handed to the newly-arrived Bracciano who, reading the passionate contents, erupts in a fury of suspicious jealousy. When Vittoria appears, he impetuously denounces the deception implied in the letter. Though her vigorous denial effects a recantation from Bracciano, for Vittoria the accusations have been too wounding. She refuses to respond to his attempts at reconciliation, reminding Bracciano of his role in her condemnation. The appeals of neither Flamineo nor Bracciano have any effect and Vittoria breaks off the conversation. The men then plan to abduct Vittoria and travel to Padua, taking Giovanni, Marcello and Cornelia with them. The general confusion caused by the death of the Pope will cover their departure.

Commentary

This scene illustrates the lovers' intense self-will and stubbornness. Jealous anger breaks out when emotions are raised and desires thwarted. Bracciano's love for Vittoria is essentially obsessive. Any hint of treachery sparks off fierce denunciation. Francisco had cunningly surmised Bracciano's vulnerability. His appeals for forgiveness are rejected. Then it is Vittoria's turn to be adamant. Anger turns to tears, then to silence and she remains unmoved by entreaty.

   This consuming love of Bracciano and Vittoria is the centre of the whole play. It has, however, been accompanied by hostility, danger, deception and murder. The episode in the house of convertites assumes a terrible irony when the lovers – meeting, as it were, for a tryst – break into highly charged antagonistic outbursts. The sordid triviality of Flamineo's jokes and his bitter little allegory of the crocodile and the bird contrast with the powerful, emotionally charged exchanges of the lovers. Their language vividly expresses the depth of their feelings and outraged sensibilities voiced at breathless speed. This continuity is achieved partly through the fluency of the speeches, but also through the arrangement of the verse. As one speech ends, so the next takes up the argument as an extension of the same line, for example:

Bracciano	Are not those matchless eyes mine?
Vittoria	I had rather
	They were not matches.
Bracciano	Is not this lip mine?
Vittoria	Yes: thus to bite off, rather than give it thee. (133-5)

No time is allowed for breath or reflection.

Act IV, Scene iii

Summary

The Vatican The cardinals engaged in the election of a new Pope are guarded by various orders of knights with Count Lodovico in attendance.

It is announced that Monticelso has been chosen, taking the title of Pope Paul IV. His first act is to excommunicate the exiles. Francisco is exultant when he is given the news. His trap has worked and Bracciano has been disgraced.

Having planned the murder of Bracciano, Francisco leaves, but the Pope has noticed his earnest conversation with Lodovico and demands to know what was proposed. The Count is severely reprimanded by the Pope when he admits his love for Isabella and his desire to avenge her murder. But a little later, receiving a gift of money from the Pope (it is actually from Francisco) he is convinced his plan has papal blessing.

Commentary

The splendid display created by the ambassadors in ceremonial uniform is made more spectacular with the acclamation surrounding the appearance of the new Pope in full regalia. Webster is referring to his historical sources by including this colourful and theatrically attractive pageant. But the play's focus quickly returns to Vittoria and Bracciano since the Pope's first act is to denounce and excommunicate them. The plot now concentrates on Francisco's obsessive pursuit of revenge with Lodovico as his accessory. The election marks a distinct change in Monticelso's attitude. In speeches that precede his final exit from the play, the new Pope makes an energetic and successful attempt to dissuade Lodovico from his murderous course. But the newly-penitent is subverted by a bribe which seems to contradict the earlier exhortation. In fact the money has been sent by the machiavellian Duke, who is ready to use the Pope as an instrument to deceive Lodovico. This supposed papal duplicity draws a forceful denunciation of misused authority from Lodovico.

Act V, Scene i

Summary

Bracciano's palace in Padua The marriage of Vittoria and Bracciano has taken place. Flamineo describes Mullinassar, a Moor and two Hungarian noblemen who are visitors at the palace. In fact, they are Francisco, Lodovico and Gasparo in disguise. Bracciano welcomes the newcomers and invites them to the tournament which is part of his wedding celebrations. The real intention of Francisco and his companions is to bring about Bracciano's murder by devious trickery. Their talk is interrupted by Flamineo bringing with him Marcello and Zanche, a Moorish maid servant. Flamineo attempts to find out more about the visitors, but Francisco will reveal little about himself.

While the knights prepare for the jousting, Zanche returns, arguing with Flamineo whose affection for her she suspects has cooled. Marcello does not approve of his brother's liaison with this dark-skinned servant girl. He and his mother, Cornelia, think her to be little more than a prostitute. Zanche is very attracted to the Moorish Mullinassar and seeks to ingratiate herself by offering to confide certain secrets to him.

Commentary

The theme dominating Act V is revenge, achieved not through direct confrontation but by trickery, deception and disguise. There is delight in deceit and the infliction of pain. The marriage of Bracciano is reported rather than presented. Horror not happiness is to be the pervasive tone of the scene. For the moment Flamineo's assured position dulls his usual wariness and he fails to penetrate Francisco's disguise. He speaks approvingly of the Moor and his two Hungarian companions, little realising who they are. Even the wily Bracciano is equally misled and welcomes the avengers into his palace. We notice how gleefully the conspirators itemise the various insidious means for poisoning Bracciano. Flamineo's conversation with his brother conducted in light-hearted terms, crudely larded with sexual imagery, reiterates his calculating use of friendship and loyalty. The notion that it must be totally self-serving revolts Marcello.

The character of Zanche becomes important in this scene. She enjoys the confidence of Vittoria; she is the current, if uneasy, lover of Flamineo and her Moorish origin connects her with the disguised Francisco. It is her suspicion of Flamineo's cooling ardour that encourages an approach to her supposed countryman. We notice Zanche's willingness to betray secrets because she has been slighted. Integrity is very lightly valued. Only Marcello and Cornelia take any moral stance, but their anger is focused principally on Zanche. They seem unaware of the larger deceits. Physical disguise, especially with such exotic costumes, intensifies the already deep-laid deceptions.

Act V, Scene ii

Summary

Bracciano's Palace Flamineo, angered by his brother's disparagement of Zanche, kills him whilst Marcello is in conversation with his mother. Cornelia cannot believe that her son is dead. The knights, preparing for the lists, find her kneeling distractedly over his body. She refuses consolation and draws a knife to stab Flamineo, but her courage fails. Whilst Bracciano is preoccupied with Cornelia, the disguised Lodovico sprinkles the face-guard of Bracciano's helmet with poison.

Commentary

This scene introduces the series of murders that occupy the concluding sequences of the play. The virtuous Marcello is the first to die, cold-bloodedly killed by an aggrieved brother. Flamineo escapes death twice – once when his mother cannot bring herself to kill her sole remaining son and later when Bracciano's admonitory sentence stops short of death. He is given a daily licence to live. Bracciano's leniency is to be his undoing. Concern for Marcello and Cornelia allows his attention to be deflected from Lodovico's surreptitious treatment of the helmet. If Flamineo sees the assassin at work he does not warn Bracciano whose forbearance gets little recompense from his resentful, outwardly obedient secretary.

Act V, Scene iii

Summary

The tournament proceeds until Bracciano enters, calling for his armourer to tear off his helmet. He realises that he has been poisoned. The frightened Giovanni is hurried away. Vittoria is refused a kiss lest she risk poisoning. Bracciano is carried into a private room by two monks, who, in fact, are Lodovico and Gasparo in disguise.

Flamineo speaks disparagingly of his master to Francisco until Bracciano is brought back on a stretcher. The dying man speaks distractedly, seeing strange visions. When he is left alone with the two monks for the administration of the last rites, the avengers reveal their true identity, curse and insult their victim. Bracciano temporarily revives and calls for Vittoria. But she is dismissed by the plotters who complete their task by strangling Bracciano. Flamineo is scornful of Vittoria's tears of anguish, but he quickly realises that he is alone, without allies.

Zanche flirts with Francisco, who is still disguised as a Moor, recounting a dream in which he seemed to sleep with her, but she also reveals the truth about Isabella's poisoning and the murder of Camillo. She was an acessory to the crimes and as a penance she determines to steal Vittoria's jewels and present them to Francisco. They plan a midnight meeting in the chapel.

Commentary

The shouts and charges of the tournament provide a noisy introduction to Bracciano's death throes. As he struggles to tear off the poisoned helmet, Bracciano is unaware that he is surrounded by enemies. With the boy Giovanni sent away and Vittoria kept at arm's length by the conspirators, the dramatic focus is totally upon Bracciano. Any doubts about Flamineo's callousness are completely removed in his commentary on the dying Bracciano and the distressed Vittoria. His service has been for entirely selfish motives and he rejects his sister's grief as superficial sorrow.

Bracciano's words contrast the sweetness of natural demise and horrific murder. Poetic death-images are associated with the screech owl, the wolf and the raven. In his distraction we are given a kaleidoscope of pictures featuring his life as a soldier and statesman. References to battle, taxes, oppression and misplaced loyalty tumble together with visions of the approaching death. Flamineo is seen as a money-grabbing tightrope-walker. The name of Vittoria is hardly mentioned. The pseudo-monks performing the rites of extreme unction with crucifix and taper, comfort Bracciano in Latin, but condemn him in brusque vernacular. Lodovico jokes about the rope with which he finally strangles Bracciano as 'a true-love knot sent of the Duke of Florence'.

The speed and momentum of the action is sustained by Zanche's revelations. While the truth concerning Isabella's murder and the promise of possessing Vittoria's riches seems to justify and satisfy Lodovico's desire for revenge, Francisco remains obsessed – the whole 'disease' must be purged.

Act V, Scene iv

Summary

The palace at Padua Flamineo finds himself rejected by the young prince, Giovanni, and ordered out of court. Cornelia has been driven mad with grief and she enters, dragging the corpse of Marcello. Her wild singing and garbled language moves Flamineo strangely. For a moment he experiences a pang of compassion. Rejected and distressed, he hopes for support from his sister but at this moment the ghost of Bracciano appears, throws earth on him and presents a skull. Flamineo realises that his only hope lies with Vittoria. If she denies him, he will murder her.

Commentary

This scene marks Flamineo's increasing isolation. His joking ripostes to the young prince are coldly received. Next, he is faced with the spectacle of his dead brother's corpse clasped by a grief-stricken, maddened mother. Then Bracciano's ghost offers inescapable symbols of death. Although for the first time, he uses words like 'compassion' and 'conscience', the sense of rejection makes him a desperate, cornered man.

The appearance of the distracted mother bears a strong resemblance to the episode in Shakespeare's *Hamlet* when mad Ophelia, garlanded in flowers, chants snatches of ribald folk songs. Cornelia's speeches draw on many common images of death – the screech owl, the cricket, the wolf –

and her funeral dirge is much like the sombre nursery rhyme 'Who killed Cock-robin?'. The simplicity of the language with its regular rhyming couplets and the strong folklore symbols offers a vivid contrast to the sophisticated language of deceit and double talk found elsewhere in the play.

Act V, Scenes v and vi

Summary
Bracciano's servant, Hortensio, overhears Lodovico and Francisco plotting further murder.

A desperate Flamineo demands reward from his sister, but she refuses him anything. Flamineo rushes out and returns immediately with a case of pistols, threatening to kill her. He claims that he made a vow to Bracciano that neither he nor Vittoria should outlive him. Vittoria's protestations and cries are of no avail. Zanche whispers to her mistress, suggesting that they appear to submit, but insist that he dies first. Flamineo agrees. Vittoria and Zanche, believing they have shot Flamineo, exult over his dying body, but he has tricked them with an assumed death. As Flamineo seeks his own retribution, Lodovico and Gasparo, still robed as monks, enter. They throw off their disguise and proceed to stab Flamineo, Vittoria and Zanche. Vittoria dies first and Flamineo shortly after her.

The disturbance has roused Giovanni and the officers, who, fearing an attack on the young prince, shoot and wound Lodovico. In his dying moments, he reveals Francisco's complicity in the murder and his presence in the palace disguised as the Moor. Giovanni asserts that the wrongdoer will be punished.

Commentary
Modern audiences find it hard to accept the theatrical contrivance that provides a sensational conclusion to the play. Perhaps recent evidence of horrifying hold-ups, murders, assassination and revenge killings reduces the apparent excesses of Webster's play. Whilst the circumstances of Vittoria's final moments relate very clearly to the death of the real-life Vittoria Accoramboni the events of the scene as a whole are Webster's own invention. Flamineo achieves a pinnacle of machiavellian deceit in tricking his sister. Finding his desperate demands rejected, he proposes a suicide pact. The aftermath of the false death exposes the most violent antagonism between brother and sister even if there is a certain joking ribaldry in the language. But the tone and mood of the scene change with the arrival of the assassins, Lodovico and his accomplices. At last Flamineo recognises the courage of his sister as she unflinchingly faces death. Vittoria's words

epitomise stoical endurance that refuses to look for false comfort. The dying Flamineo speaks of the vanity of the world, his last words containing an ironic joke. We notice that young Giovanni gives short shrift to Lodovico. The closing couplet insists that wrongs committed for whatever reason will be punished. The malcontent whose dissatisfied grumbling opened the play now finds himself condemned to torture and imprisonment. The final irony is that the pair who seem to escape retribution within the play are the new Pope and Duke Francisco. The real power-lords are not displaced.

3 THEMES

3.1 LUST AND LOYALTY

The fierce passion that unites Vittoria and Bracciano stands at the centre
of the play. The nature of that relationship, however, is predominantly
sexual rather than compassionate. It is closer to lust than love. Though
they become man and wife, we do not witness wedded bliss. Far from it,
the marriage ceremony is but a prelude to the revenge killings. Vittoria
speaks few lines at Bracciano's assassination and he seems ignorant of his
wife's presence. Bracciano's name is not even mentioned at Vittoria's
death. Webster directs our attention much more firmly to their earlier
relationship when we see mutual passion that defies convention and can
accommodate treacherous murder. The victims, Isabella and Camillo, are
ruthlessly dispatched without the slightest hint of remorse. There might
be some blame attached to Isabella for her unexplained absence and her
quick remonstrance, but nothing could warrant the cruel poisoning of the
picture. The essentially simple, if foolishly trusting, Camillo is killed without
compunction. Admiration for the intensity of Vittoria's and Bracciano's
sensual passion must be seriously modified if any kind of moral judgement is applied. They defy convention by committing adultery; they
challenge the law with the arranged murders. They remain completely
unmoved at their victims' fate. Vittoria is ready to use Flamineo as a
pander and he is equally willing to betray his brother-in-law in favour of
his master. Any kind of family loyalty is hard to find. For Flamineo, the
opportunist, the love between Vittoria and Bracciano is seen as a chance
to advance his own prospects. His brother, Marcello, and their mother,
Cornelia, who show at least some signs of integrity, are treated with disdain.
Marcello is murdered by his brother and Cornelia driven mad by her
murderous son. Morality and family loyalty fail against selfishness and lust.
The consuming love of Vittoria and Bracciano compulsively overrides all
objections and obstacles regardless of cost. This mutual selfishness and

restricted concept of loyalty challenge the very fabric of society. But if we look at the upholders of that society's standards, we find equally relentless personal selfishness. Francisco, Duke of Florence, who should support moral standards, is shown to be a villain. Cardinal Monticelso possesses a black book of villains ready to carry out his evil intentions.

Rebellion is set within an unjust society where the fittest and most astute survive. Love is essentially equated with lust and loyalty comes very low in the list of priorities of family relationships.

3.2 AMBITION

Bracciano's desire for Vittoria could be seen as an example of the ambition to possess. His methods certainly identify a relentless pursuit of a desired goal. Flamineo's ambition to acquire position and influence is for self-advancement at whatever cost. He sees Vittoria – for whose reputation he cares little – as a pawn in the game. He readily breaks Camillo's neck and allows Vittoria to take the blame because he feels assured of the powerful Bracciano's protection. He treats the trial as a light-hearted escapade, laughs at Marcello's misgivings and shows little compassion for Vittoria when she is condemned. His sister calls him a pander when he attempts a reconciliation with Bracciano during the episode of the trick-letter. For Flamineo, ambition overrides loyalty, responsibility and trust. But successful advancement depends on his employer and with Bracciano's death Flamineo is immediately vulnerable. His selfish aspirations for power and position dissolve into a sordid death. He becomes the victim of the Machiavellian deceit by which he had hoped to become great.

3.3 REVENGE AND RETRIBUTION

The typical revenge tragedies of the Jacobean period featured a victim, demonstrably wronged, seeking retribution on his assailant. Here the emphasis is on retribution, or retaliation by unsuspected assailants such as Lodovico, the *secret* admirer of Isabella or the malicious vengeance of Francisco, her brother. Isabella makes a relatively brief appearance in the play before she is poisoned by the 'fum'd' picture, but her impact is sufficient to instigate a double revenge theme that is sustained through the whole play. Webster creates Lodovico as a disgruntled nobleman complaining of unjust treatment, but his resentment lies in Vittoria's failure to secure his pardon. Only in the dumb show do we learn of his infatuation with Isabella, but this becomes the chief spur for his personal vendetta. We notice that Lodovico and Isabella never meet in the play, so that

Webster's chief concern is with the process of retribution rather than portraying a secret love-affair between Lodovico and Isabella.

Lodovico's position is greatly strengthened by his appointment as Giovanni's guardian, money bequeathed by Isabella and the pardon obtained from the Pope by the intervention of Francisco. This removes from him any necessity to ally himself with Flamineo. He also gains an influential position at the Papal election, again, no doubt, through the influence of the Duke. So he is ready to serve Francisco's purposes in murdering Bracciano since it also meets his own desire to avenge Isabella's death. He further justifies his murderous intention through the models of deceit apparently provided by the new Pope. Retribution for Lodovico is achieved using deception and disguise rather than direct personal confrontation. For all except Flamineo he is an unsuspected avenger. But he remains unsatisfied by Bracciano's death. Revenge has become a personal obsession. It cannot be claimed that his banishment or his infatuation for Isabella offers a just foundation for retribution. Yet he relentlessly pursues his objective using influence, deceit, trickery, disguise and personal violence. He justifies his actions by quoting the absence of any general rule of justice, the poor examples of his betters and the obvious success of oppressive power. Whilst denouncing the world's deceits, he fails to recognise the deceptions played on him, notably by the Duke of Florence, for whom he becomes a hired assassin. His triumph in revenge is shortlived. Giovanni condemns the 'bloody villain'. His previous position as guardian carries no weight and he is sentenced to torture on the rack, though, Lodovico does see a final glory in his achievement and speaks contemptuously of forthcoming punishment. Retribution in Lodovico's case is a matter of personal revenge for not wholly admirable reasons. His final condemnation can be seen as a just conclusion to a life of murder, corruption, deceit and violence.

Whilst Francisco has the same impulse to revenge as Lodovico, his method of operation is entirely different. He seems to escape final punishment, even if Giovanni, for whom Francisco was an apparently indulgent uncle, does order his apprehension. Francisco employs agents for his nefarious purposes, which removes the necessity for his personal engagement in violence. The Duke exhibits considerable political acumen in his unscrupulous use of influential colleagues such as Monticelso. Throughout the trial, Francisco keeps a low profile, leaving the Cardinal to lead the attack. Afterwards he seems to temporise with Bracciano. The new Pope is persuaded to excommunicate the runaway lovers. The naive Camillo is used as a decoy to tempt Bracciano to further adultery. But most significantly, Francisco sees in the obsessed Lodovico an admirable instrument for his own revenge. At the poisoning of the helmet, Francisco, disguised as Mullinassar, merely looks on. By taking advantage of Zanche's flirtatious approaches, the Duke learns the precise details of Isabella's and Camillo's deaths and gains the chance to appropriate Vittoria's jewels and money. Then he withdraws from the action before the final assassinations begin.

Webster explores the theme of retribution through these two contrasted examples. We feel little sympathy for either since their motives are suspect and their methods distasteful. One receives summary punishment, the other appears to escape – at least within the play. Webster shows retribution less as an intention to redress injustice than as a consuming, personal passion. Claims for justice or justification have a hollow ring. We cannot differentiate between the actions of the avenger and the wrongs of the accused – all are marked by personal obsessiveness, a readiness to deceive and a willingness to kill. Far from regarding these obsessions as horrific and despicable, society seems to accept such behaviour as normal and acceptable. Only in the young Giovanni's closing speech does there seem a faint hope of justice and fair dealing in the future.

4 INTERPRETATIONS

Whilst it is relatively easy to identify the principal themes, the question of their relationship to an overall interpretation of the play remains. One point of view suggests that it is merely sensational theatre designed to shock and horrify, but saved by the splendour of the poetry. Others see the play as strongly moralistic, where the audience is invited to condemn rather than admire. A third way interprets the play as a comment on contemporary Jacobean society based on real events but distanced by its Italian setting.

4.1 DECADENT SENSATIONAL THEATRICALITY

The poisoning of Isabella, Camillo's broken neck, the horrific throes of a dying tormented Bracciano, the bloody shoot-out ending in the death of Vittoria, Zanche and Flamineo and Lodovico's wounding suggest sensationalism introduced for theatrical effect with little regard to reality. Certainly the scenes in performance make a powerful impression on the stage. But Webster intentionally distances the first two murders from us by displaying them in dumb show. They are played out, as it were, in slow motion, so that we are intrigued by the method as well as shocked by the effect. Only when we are well into the play and more conversant with the corrupt society that is portrayed do we see the actual murder of Bracciano. But it should be noted that Webster did not invent the mode of Bracciano's death, spectacular though it may seem. It is likely that he utilised a report of such a killing by a Florentine knight (see *Revels* edn, p. 141). Reality can be sensational. We have seen far too many examples of stabbings, shootings and carnage that erupt within a supposedly peaceful society. Whilst in the past, we have asserted that such horrors were unbelievable, events have shown them to be only too real and possible. It is the overingeniousness of the pistols episode that makes it seem incredible rather than the arrangement of the macabre suicide pact.

The tempestuous love-affair between Vittoria and Bracciano accompanied by such acts of violence might also invite the label sensational. But if we look at the basic historical facts, the real Bracciano and Vittoria were desperately in love and Vittoria was assassinated by one Lodovico. Only Bracciano died from natural causes – an ulcerous leg infection. No sensational love scenes are presented on the stage. Though Webster conveys the undoubted depth of their passion, we also see the lovers at odds, suspicious and angry with each other. There is a reality about their relationship that cannot simply be described as theatrical sensationalism. Too many modern instances remind us of the frailty of marriage and the flaring violence that frequently accompanies such breakdowns.

4.2 A SENSE OF MORALITY

Lord David Cecil wrote of Webster: 'His vision is a moral one. Each play presents us with a picture of an act of sin and its consequences' (R. V. Holdsworth (ed.), *Webster: The White Devil and The Duchess of Malfi* (London, 1984) p.66). This view of the play contrasts sharply with the one that dismisses *The White Devil* as sensational theatricality. How is this moral vision presented? There are no really significant upholders of morality in the play. Young Giovanni's final admonition:

Let guilty men remember their black deeds
Do lean on crutches made of slender reeds. (V.v. 89-90)

makes a conventionally moral observation, but we see little of the justice of which he speaks operating within the play. Isabella's fidelity to her husband expressed in the adoration of his picture, is the immediate cause of her death. Cornelia is driven mad when her innocent son is stabbed by his brother. Camillo is such a light-weight character that he does not offer any substantial moral example. He is too trusting, too easily duped. Vigour of action and depth of character are most vividly displayed by what might be called the 'bad' characters. However much he may shock us by their duplicity and audacity, Webster seldom invites us to admire these figures. Political and religious leaders who should personify integrity, in fact present selfishness, ambition and machiavellian deceit. No single action of Duke Francisco or Cardinal Monticelso is held up for approval. Though both avoid retribution, in neither case does that escape give pleasure or win approbation. Both invite moral condemnation as examples of a corrupt world. The relentless desire to succeed that Flamineo represents is ambition that destroys. He is pander to his sister, slayer of his brother and bane to his mother. He devalues human affection and family loyalty. He begins as the favoured secretary to Bracciano and ends as an outcast, rejected by his sister as a villain. Lodovico's obsession similarly brings about his condemnation. Flamineo's death and Lodovico's arrest are the natural consequences of their sinful lives.

The case of Bracciano and Vittoria is more complex. Whilst they are linked as lovers, their conduct in the play is quite distinctive. Bracciano happily uses his secretary as a go-between, is elated by the plans to murder Isabella and Camillo. His behaviour at Vittoria's trial is less than noble. He deserts her at the moment of her greatest need and even negotiates with her accusers. He is easily tricked by the false letter. His quickness to condemn is only equalled by the alacrity of his contrition and anger at its rejection. Neither gullibility nor quick temper are qualities to be admired. As Bracciano was ready to deceive and destroy Isabella and Camillo, so he is deceived and destroyed by Francisco and Lodovico. He is poisoned and strangled as Isabella was poisoned and Camillo's neck was broken. Evil matches evil. For Vittoria the picture is somewhat different, although she is the 'white devil' of the title. A good deal of sympathy is raised for her especially at the trial when the principal of-fender, Bracciano, is not in the dock but present as an observer who interrupts but does not sustain his support. Marcello is rightly excused, but Flamineo, the actual killer, is also absolved. There is manifest in-justice in the ludicrous Latinisation of the lawyer and when the judge becomes the accuser. Vittoria may be an adulteress but she is not, at this point, a murderess. As Vittoria asserts: 'Justice has been ravished'. We must admire her energetic and spirited defence of her actions and recog-nise the isolation in which she is left when lover and brother, more con-cerned for themselves, are silent on her behalf. There is little happiness in her short-lived marriage. Her trickery with Flamineo in the suicide pact is equal to Flamineo's but neither is genuinely successful. There is bravery in her defiance but we are aware that her dying words, condemning the profligate selfishness of court life, apply most strongly to Vittoria herself. As she sowed, so did she reap.

The picture that Webster paints is not one in which exultant amorality flourishes, riding roughshod over all opposition, but a sombre, pessimistic assessment of an unjust society where passion, ambition, hatred and greed project the protagonists along paths of destruction culminating in their own deaths. Nowhere is approval voiced of that society. A stern moral code is illustrated through numerous examples of what happens when that code is breached. The play is an exposure of evil not its cele-bration.

4.3 A SENSE OF REALITY

The basic plot of *The White Devil* was derived from a factual account of
the life and death of Vittoria Accoramboni, married to Francesco Peretti
(Camillo in the play) who was nephew to Cardinal Montalto (Monticelso
in the play). Her affair with the Duke of Bracciano was notorious in
Italy. He married Vittoria secretly after her husband had been murdered.
Pope Gregory disallowed the marriage. Vittoria was imprisoned after
investigations into Peretti's death. After her release, she remarried Bracciano.
Shortly after the appointment of Pope Sextus (Paul in the play) Vittoria
and Bracciano escaped to Padua but Bracciano died in the same year from
physical infirmity. The relatives of Bracciano's first wife tried to gain
possession of his wealth in the course of which Vittoria was murdered by
Lodovico Orsini (Lodovico in the play). These were the bare bones of the
story that Webster came to know through a variety of sources, none of
which gave the full facts. The account of Vittoria's daring relationship
with Bracciano and her own murder was not Webster's invention but real
and recent historical fact (Vittoria was born in 1557 and died 1585 or 6).

In a recent and informative book *John Webster: Citizen and Dramatist*
M. Bradbrook traces the adventures of Penelope Rich, daughter of the
Earl of Essex and her affair with Charles Blount, soldier, scholar and
courtier to King James. Their relationship intrigued, if it did not scanda-
lise, London and the Court which Webster knew well. Miss Bradbrook
records that when Penelope eventually married Blount who had already
fathered five sons, the King commented 'a fair woman with a black soul'.
Not exactly the 'white devil', but the parallels are sufficiently striking for
the play to offer an impressive contemporary model for the characters
of Vittoria and Bracciano. Penelope and Blount indulged in continuous
intrigues, plots and assignations involving her brother, the Earl of Essex;
her husband, Lord Rich; and her lover. Even her mother, Lettice Knollys,
a formidable figure in Court, was deeply implicated. Thus the atmosphere
of intrigue and plotting in *The White Devil* found many similarities in the
complicated machinations of the English Court at the turn of the century
when the Tudor Queen Elizabeth (reign 1558-1603) was succeeded by
the Stuart King James I (reign, 1603-25). A sense of reality is reinforced
in the play by this knowledge that material for the drama was not derived
from a fanciful imagination, but based on observation of how people in
real life actually behaved. Webster's characters achieve realistic intensity
by absorbing qualities possessed by known historical figures.

5 TECHNICAL FEATURES

5.1 PLOT AND STRUCTURE

The conventional five acts into which the play is divided do not really identify either the plot or the actual structure of the drama. The story itself falls into three distinct parts, each of which is only loosely connected in terms of plot development. The first explores the love affair between Bracciano and Vittoria. Their liaison is aided and abetted by Flamineo who willingly dupes his brother-in-law, Camillo, and upbraids his mother when she threatens to interfere. Having established the disjunction between Vittoria and the foolish Camillo, and the break between Bracciano and his wife, Webster introduces the authority figures of Monticelso and Francisco as determined antagonists. There is no doubt about the inherent danger of the relationship between the two lovers. The second part concentrates on Vittoria's trial when accusations of prostitution, adultery and murder are flung at her. The speeches consist of long denunciations with slight supporting evidence. She is given little opportunity to respond. Bracciano plays only a minor part in the trial. His intervention is brief, peremptory and ineffective. The only factual evidence offered is an intercepted love-letter containing money. This is interpreted as a sign of Vittoria's guilt despite her protestations and she is immediately sentenced. Bracciano and Flamineo avoid condemnation though they are actually the guilty parties.

The third part of the plot revolves around Francisco's revenge for the death of his sister. Chronologically there is a long time-gap, but the stage events flow swiftly forward. No hints of Francisco's future intentions were given when he heard of Isabella's death, other than an expression of grief and a desire to keep her memory fresh. The third part turns that grief into a violent intent to kill, encouraged by Monticelso and abetted by Lodovico. The plan is achieved by the play's conclusion through a series of machiavellian deceits – a trick love-letter, a poisoned helmet, murderers disguised as Franciscan monks and hired assassins. Interposed between those events is the story of the increasingly desperate Flamineo. His death, coinciding with that of his sister, brings the two threads of the plot together in a rather abrupt conclusion which suggests the re-establishment of justice in the figure of young Giovanni.

The play's somewhat loose structure does not reduce the overall impact which is derived, not from a carefully plotted series of sequential episodes each carefully dovetailing into the next, but, from a range of vividly dramatic, self-contained scenes connected by the characters who commonly inhabit them. A particularly strong example is the arraignment of Vittoria. From a previous scene we know that Flamineo and Marcello have been arrested in connection with the death of Camillo. The trial however does not deal with the indictment of Flamineo and Marcello as we might expect. Rather does it concentrate on the defects of the moral character of Vittoria.

This is what occupies the major part of the scene. The death of Camillo is used as an *excuse* for Vittoria's arrest and the trial represents a considerable change of emphasis. The real facts are not the concern of this court, instead the accusers are out for Vittoria's blood. The trial setting, the fierce argument and Vittoria's resistance make the scene a compelling one to watch. The death of Camillo lies unresolved until much later in the play, and Isabella's poisoning, which the audience knows to have taken place, receives no mention until the trial is over. Even then no suspicions are voiced about her death. The logical sequence of events should include an investigation of the deaths. Webster chooses another and more compelling focus that develops the character of Vittoria in such a way as to contrast with what we already know of her as a dissatisfied wife and eager adulteress.

Strictly speaking the election of Monticelso to the Papal chair is not an essential scene in *The White Devil* but it offers a brilliant occasion visually. Monticelso's known disgust with the lovers now receives papal endorsement. Central to the scene is the excommunication. No more potent demonstration could be given of the animosity that the runaways have brought upon their heads. Theatrically splendid and awesome though the scene may be it must be remembered that it was based on an historical fact. An important element of reality is contained in an episode of pomp and ceremony. This variety of individually brilliant and dramatic scenes combines to convey the intense hazards that Vittoria and Bracciano face in their passionate love affair. Their deaths are portrayed in equally dramatic, self-contained scenes.

5.2 CHARACTERISATION

Vittoria

With the title *The White Devil*, we cannot expect a virtuous heroine at the centre of the play. She is not a fiendlike queen such as Lady Macbeth, but she is an encourager of and accessory to murder. Where is the 'white' aspect of her character? M. C. Bradbrook describes her personality as a 'reconciliation of opposites'. Undoubtedly she is a great physical beauty, unappreciated by her husband, magnetically attractive to Bracciano. It is not surprising that Vittoria should seek a more exciting companion than her dull Camillo. We may not approve of, but cannot discount, the intensity of these lovers' passion for each other. At the arraignment, the corruptness of the proceedings, the bias of the accusers and the escape of the actual murderers contrast strongly with Vittoria's spirited defence as an isolated prisoner. We actually see her taking her punishment in the convent, whilst Bracciano and Flamineo remain free. Suffering condemnation from a hasty and unthinking lover, she rightly exclaims, emphasising her isolation and ill-treatment, 'What have I gained by thee but infamy'. Her dearly-bought marriage is short-lived and she is forced to watch her husband's death agonies unable to offer comfort or remedy. Her marriage home has become a 'place of hell'. In her final appearance, Vittoria bruised and saddened by her experiences, faces the demands of a brother whose villainy has now become plain. At least one of her enemies can be destroyed. But it is not to be. Though Flamineo outwits and deceives her, the avenging Lodovico brings death in his wake and Vittoria is murdered. Her courage and spirit dominate the proceedings and we are left with a sense of a woman fighting in a man's world, suffering more and punished more severely than those whose guilt is greater.

Bracciano

As Vittoria displays a double identity, so does Bracciano. The part he plays is full of ambiguities so that our feelings move between approval and distaste. We recognise his besotted love for Vittoria which overwhelms his judgement. Isabella's cool and critical attitude suggests an unhappy marriage from which anyone might wish to escape. Yet the employment of a pander like Flamineo and a magician like the conjuror reveals a single-minded selfishness pursued regardless of the pain it creates for others and the blame that might be attached to the innocent. His gleeful enjoyment of the conjuration and his swift departure following the arrest of Marcello, Flamineo and Vittoria suggest over-concern for his own skin. He bribes his way into Vittoria's trial. Since he is her only ally, he might be expected to be vigorous in her defence. Instead he remains silent while Vittoria is being abused and only joins in when his own reputation might be at risk.

He offers a plausible excuse for his presence in the house on the night of the murder. Far from sustaining support for Vittoria he breaks into an angry altercation with Monticelso and storms out uttering threats. As Monticelso ironically and tersely remarks to Vittoria 'Your champion's gone'. The trial scene and the subsequent overtures of friendship made to Francisco damage our view of Bracciano as an urgent, concerned lover. In the house of convertites, Bracciano condemns Vittoria as 'a stately and advanced whore', a 'devil in crystal'. Equally swift is his recantation together with the expectation that Vittoria will respond immediately. Here Bracciano reveals a mercurial temperament whose fast-changing emotions take little account of other people's feelings. He is indeed a selfish lover. The plan for Vittoria's abduction is made without consulting her. That Vittoria accepts the plan shows the compelling depth of her love. That Bracciano's suspicions are not roused by the Moorish Mulinassar indicates too great a self-assurance which results in retribution swiftly and fatally exacted. The joyful, spiteful deception of the disguised Lodovico and Gasparo revolts us, when Bracciano's maddened, pain-ridden words show him the victim of vicious antagonists. He expires in a welter of malevolent abuse. We have little respect for his accusers and Bracciano's awful death invites our sympathy because we actually witness the full ferocity of his murder.

Webster creates in Bracciano a character at once volatile, loving and suspicious, whose moods change abruptly from softness to anger. His love for Vittoria is an urgent dynamic force driving him to brutal and deceptive action. With his move to Padua and his marriage to Vittoria he thought he had become invulnerable. That over-confidence brought about his downfall.

The Machiavellians
To describe Flamineo as single-minded is perhaps odd, since deceit and deviation are the principal methods by which he pursues his ambitious course. His goal is quite clear. He wants to advance his status to the highest possible rank, acquiring such richness and property as he can to sustain him in his superiority. He never deviates from that resolution even when this involves acting as pander to his sister, murderer of both her husband and his own brother and attempted killer of his sister and her maid. He seldom exhibits any compassion or regard for others, but is essentially selfish, sadistically ingenious and concerned only for his own personal safety. In language and attitude he shows a base, scurrilous view of life, seeing his fellows as lustful, ambitious, devoid of any fine or sensitive feelings. Those few characters from whom any positive moral position emerges are treated as misguided fools. This deviousness might be described as machiavellian with the ends justifying the means. His

concealed and callous selfishness is particularly exposed in relation to Vittoria. He encourages her adultery in order to secure himself in Bracciano's good books. He regards their love as animal lust. He is quick to intervene in the convent scene when it seems that his sister's resistance might imperil his position as secretary. He abuses Zanche's love for him, relegating it to veniality and convenience. She is kicked and beaten without his intervention. Flamineo's ability in quick deception is never in doubt. Camillo falls for the vaulting-horse trick. In adopting the role of madman he avoids awkward questions. His capricious disregard for his family is best illustrated in the stabbing of Marcello. No doubt he had been angered by his brother's derogatory remarks, but there is no justification for the sudden, unexpected attack. However, the sudden death of his employer leaves Flamineo very much exposed. Hoping to ingratiate himself, he denigrates Bracciano before the disguised Francisco, but his isolation is heightened by Giovanni's edict banning him from court. We witness a brief moment of compassion at his mother's madness and he speaks of 'a maze of conscience'. However, this is shortlived and his desperate, machiavellian mind turns to his sister with plans for a fake death. Success is very brief and he dies uttering a jibing curse, desiring thunder, not tolling bells, to accompany his death. In Flamineo, Webster has created a thoroughly disreputable, sardonic, quick-tongued, dirty minded careerist, whose overweening selfishness eventually destroys him.

An altogether more sophisticated Machiavellian is found in Francisco who appears to be a devoted brother to Isabella and an indulgent uncle to Giovanni. His severity with Bracciano is only to be expected. But that image changes when he uses Camillo as bait to trap Bracciano. In the arraignment scene his animosity against Vittoria and Bracciano is skilfully cloaked. In fact he almost appears as a fair-minded judge. He preserves this view by maintaining a low profile, allowing Monticelso to take over the prosecution. Even when we learn of Isabella's death, his response is not revenge but blessed remembrance.

When his desire for revenge breaks the surface, he does not operate directly but through agents like the villains in the Cardinal's black book. Whilst bemoaning 'the corrupted use some make of books', he readily employs the disgruntled Lodovico and is ready with the fake love-letter to ensnare Bracciano. His final deception is to insinuate himself disguised into the palace at Padua, there to oversee, but not participate in, the murder of Bracciano. There is a fine irony in Flamineo describing the deceits of the Duke of Florence as the 'rare tricks of a Machiavellian' to his disguised visitor Mulinassar. How true – at no time are Francisco's hands marked with blood. He takes advantage of Zanche's revelations to sequester Vittoria's property and leaves the city before the moment that Vittoria is cut down. Of all the assassins, he is the only one remaining free at the play's end. The villainy of Francisco is always cloaked either in words or an alleged concern for public morality. He uses agents and adopts physical disguise when appropriate. His villainy contrasts strongly with that of Flamineo's whose ambition consists of a career of actual violence and murder.

The third Machiavellian is Monticelso. M. Bradbrook writes: 'the Cardinal exemplifies precisely the worst kind of White Devil. . . the hypocritical churchman, the Judas of the faith'. (*John Webster: Citizen and Dramatist* (London, 1980) p.132). His reprimands against lechery, his denunciation of whoredom suggest a churchman upholding high and severe moral standards. His words are sharp, considered, perhaps too critical. His sentence, however is based on the slightest, unsubstantiated evidence without hearing any full defence. He uses his position as Cardinal to employ bullying tactics which none except Vittoria rejects. Monticelso's proposals to Francisco concerning revenge are anything but Christian and his catalogue of criminals indicates shameless use of secret corruption. Even Francisco is shocked by the knaves, bawds and murderers that the Church has assembled to carry out its villainies. With his elevation to the Papal throne, Monticelso loses not a moment in denouncing Bracciano and Vittoria. No sooner has he pronounced his formal blessings and remission of sins than he announces his act of excommunication. It is extremely difficult to accept at face value the new Pope's remonstrance to Lodovico. Its quick negation by Francisco's trick allows Lodovico's bitter observations. The Duke is not afraid to abuse his friendship with the Pope. There is no honour among 'Machiavels'.

These three characters epitomise all that is deceitful, hypocritical and cruel. They are totally devoid of any compassion or humanity. Power, ambition or revenge orders their attitude to life. Flamineo trades on other people's frailties. Francisco uses underlings to accomplish his vicious revenge. Monticelso abuses his position and power in the church, presenting a saintly moral outside to disguise corruption and villainy inside.

Vittoria's family

Apart from Flamineo, who has scant regard for family loyalty, Vittoria's family do offer a view of life that contradicts the self-seeking power lords. But the weight of their impact is slight. Although he is arrested, we know Marcello was not an accessory to Camillo's murder. We are a little surprised that his extreme criticism of Zanche leads him to attack her physically. But this unwise action provokes a fearful response from his brother. 'Virtuous Marcello' becomes another victim caught in the sinister machinations, ineffectual in his naivety. The case of Cornelia is somewhat different. She makes very apparent her condemnation of Bracciano and Vittoria's love affair even though Flamineo reproaches her in the coarsest language. Cornelia does establish a moral stance despite the fact that her words have little effect. Her condemnation of Zanche leads to painful consequences as she is forced to witness the death of her younger son, and this grief drives her mad. For Cornelia the moral tragedy lies in the disintegration of her own family. The one child with positive values is destroyed and the other recklessly rejects her advice. Despite their ineffectuality, this group does at least hint at a sense of honour and family pride that cannot be ignored.

5.3 STYLE AND LANGUAGE

In *John Webster's Borrowing* (1960) R. W. Dent comments: 'Excepting Shakespeare he was the most impressive dramatist of his day. Excepting no one he was its most impressive borrower'. Most editions of Webster's plays are crowded with footnotes indicating that a word, phrase, sentence or quotation had its origin in another piece of writing and that Webster borrowed the words to put into his own text. Estimates have suggested that up to three-quarters of his plays consist of such borrowings. This activity might be called plagiarism, or stealing, and we find the accusation levelled against Webster of being a 'word pirate'. He certainly made extensive use of other authors, not only classical but also contemporary like Shakespeare, John Donne and Sir Philip Sydney. This evidence suggests that Webster kept a 'commonplace' book in which he recorded any words, phrases or speeches that took his fancy. He was particularly attracted by proverbs or moral comments contained in brief maxims or longer fables. Commentators have delighted in researching their sources and identifying the originals. Even now it is claimed that many remain undiscovered. An implication from this borrowing might suggest that Webster is a second-rate writer, lacking imagination and invention to create his own expressions, depending on other people's ideas and inspirations. But this view is not widely held. M. Bradbrook comments that his writing represents 'a transformation of other men's phrases into something rich and strange'. (John Webster: *Citizen and Dramatist* (London, 1980) p.6). In other words, Webster does not simply repeat the words that he has borrowed, but refines the phrasing, even reversing the meaning and adjusting the poetic quality and rhythm of the borrowed material giving it freshness and originality. His texts therefore seem new rather than cobbled-up sections of old plays, poems and stories. Indeed part of Webster's reputation as a writer lies in this peculiar facility for creating a distinctive poetic style, particularly effective in performance, from the ventures of other writers. We tend to admire rather than condemn these borrowings.

Imagery

We need to look at Webster's use of imagery from two points of view – first its wide-ranging variety and second the combination of images that creates a complex and often ironic style. The vigorous impact of the opening scene provides a suitable introduction to Webster's method. Imagery from the animal kingdom which the playwright regularly employs, is represented unpleasantly by the hungry wolf and sheep cut to pieces and less threateningly by exotic caviare (sturgeon roe) and the very rare phoenix. Yet both groups contribute to a portrait of degenerate, vindictive man. The wolf and the sheep are obviously villain and victim but the prodigal feasts featuring caviare and the phoenix are made to represent bribery and corruption. Added to these are meteors, thunder and earthquake which further intensify the destructive element. A horrible medical image shows how men have been ruined by swallowing *mumia* (embalmed flesh) and vomiting it into the gutter. All these diverse images relate to a single, central idea – the way Lodovico has pursued a life of vicious destructiveness, abusing friendship and loyalty. Murder in his view is but a 'flea-bite'. The same section yields examples of Webster's borrowed *sententiae* or moral maxims. 'Fortune's a right whore' is derived from 'Fortune is fickle'. But the weak 'is fickle' is strengthened and made harsher by the substitution of 'a right whore.' 'This well goes with two buckets' is probably adapted from an epigram by a fellow-playwright, Heywood. Then there is a more extended reference to fruit trees and perfume. This has been traced in a book *Dial of Princes*, translated by Thomas North where a similar extended image is developed. In the space of only sixty lines, we find crammed together animal and weather metaphors, epigrams, images of gross appetite and proverbial sayings, several of which are borrowed. Yet it is possible to discern a coherence in that diversity which discloses the vigour of Webster's writing style. Lodovico's opening declaration denounces injustice, not because he takes a moral stance, but because he is personally aggrieved. Violent imagery taken from the animal world, the thunder and earthquake, and destructive appetite portrays an awesome picture of a corrupt world where the rich flourish by cruelty and deception and the unfortunate receive 'the world's alms' by being 'fleeced' and then sacrificed.

Set speeches and allegories

Perhaps because of his legal training, Webster is very conscious of the dramatic effect of the set speech. In Vittoria's trial, the arraignment is treated humorously in the lawyer's windy, interrupted, jargon-ridden address to the judges. But this is followed by Monticelso's lengthy denunciation of whoredom expounded through a relentless recitation of images: whores are sweetmeats, poisoned perfumes, wreckers, Russian winters, worse than exorbitant taxes, tolling bells, extortioners, worse than surgeon's cadavers or counterfeit coins. Each example is separated by the refrain 'What is a whore?'. The juxtaposition of the expected and unexpected, the continual piling up of metaphors and similes, each more distasteful than the last, gives the speech a forceful rhetorical flow inviting condemnation and disgust at the trade of prostitution. In contrast we notice the brevity of Vittoria's reply, 'This character escapes me'. She is not frightened by 'glass hammers' and 'painted devils'. Another literary device that Webster uses, particularly with Flamineo, is the elaborate description or allegory in prose. It may be a reminiscence of a love-intrigue, an old tale of trick spectacles or an ambiguous allegory about crocodiles. These passages give a different pace and tone from the sharp whirlwind exchanges of accusation and counter-accusation, tempering and varying the overall verbal style of the scene.

Irony and humour
Flamineo is the chief exponent. His stories often depend on irony for their humour. They may involve enjoyment of duplicity or mockery of the foolish but we are nevertheless forced to laugh at his brisk, black-humoured raillery. Most of the humour is concerned with ridicule. Flamineo is particularly sharp on Camillo. He recites a whole string of epithets to describe the unfortunate man – 'so unable to please a woman that like a Dutch doublet all his back is shrunk into his breeches' (a sign of impotency). Usually there is some sexual innuendo in Flamineo's observation so his humour is frequently crude. The joking becomes wilder and more extreme when he adopts insanity as a protective barrier. Even his death is described as 'an everlasting cold'. The irony and humour catches us by its daring or shock effects.

5.4 STAGECRAFT

Realism and convention
The White Devil does not represent a straightforward dramatisation of the real Vittoria Accoramboni legend – indeed we are not sure how much of the story Webster actually knew. The realistic historical events are absorbed into the play using many of the conventions of contemporary Jacobean theatre. Audiences would be familiar with these conventions and accept as commonplaces that which we might find incredible, horrific or excessively theatrical. The use of such devices as dumb shows, ghosts, religious rites, symbolic dreams, real and feigned madness, elaborate disguise, and sensational death scenes prevent The White Devil being received as an historical re-enactment. The careful combination of thea-

trical convention and realism displays Webster's dramatic skill. He uses theatrical devices to illustrate real events. For example, the mimetic deaths of Isabella and Camillo echo the real fate of their historical predecessors. The splendid election and denunciation scene with the new Pope accurately records an historical fact. The author uses theatrical spectacle to underline historical veracity.

The trials, ceremonies, elections and tournaments add grandeur and visual splendour to a play that might otherwise have been a series of devious, private plots. The presence of the influential ambassadors at the trial and probably the tournament, emphasises the importance of those events. Vittoria and Bracciano are seen to occupy a very public stage. Webster also makes clever dramatic use of the conventional revenge-play ghost. Francisco is visited by his sister's ghost. Her appearance is evoked by his desires and encourages him to seek active retribution. It is a turning-point in Francisco's attitude from reflection to action. Bracciano's ghost serves a completely different purpose. He is a ghostly *memento mori*, foretelling destruction with his emblems of death. This ghost drives Flamineo to even more desperate lengths to secure his future.

The whole play is shot through with deception. But the deceit by which Francisco triumphs is a disguise so effective that it is never penetrated. The full impact of this daring and effective device is recognised only when it is seen on the stage. We see Zanche deceived by the strange, exotically dressed, mysterious strangers. The murder of Bracciano by the disguised monks makes a powerful visual impression, especially since the victim fails to recognise his adversaries.

Revenge-plays of this period were noted for their savagery with multiple deaths and excess of blood. We should observe, however, that Webster reserves the violence for a short section of the final act. The deaths of Camillo and Isabella are displayed in dumb show, distancing them from reality. Marcello's death is made tragic by the grief of his maddened mother. With Bracciano's death it is the cunning deception and Bracciano's distracted speeches that impel our attention. The trick suicide-pact which stretches our credulity is over very quickly and only then does real horror erupt. This, again, is short-lived, brought to an abrupt end by Giovanni's severe dispensation of justice. Webster manages the violence so that it gradually intensifies, culminating in a brief episode of destruction. The play is not simply a series of bloody murders.

6 SPECIMEN PASSAGE AND COMMENTARY

THE WHITE DEVIL

Act II, scene ii

    Enter BRACCIANO *with one in the habit of a Conjurer*

BRACCIANO Now sir I claim your promise – 'tis dead midnight;
    The time prefix'd to show me by your art
    How the intended murder of Camillo,
    And our loathed duchess grow to action.

CONJUROR You have won me by your bounty to a deed
    I do not often practise – some there are,
    Which by sophistic tricks, aspire that name
    Which I would gladly lose, of nigromancer;
    As some that use to juggle upon cards,
    Seeming to conjure, when indeed they cheat:
    Others that raise up their confederate spirits
    'Bout windmills, and endanger their own necks,
    For making of a squib, and some there are
    Will keep a curtal to show juggling tricks
    And give out 'tis a spirit: besides these
    Such a whole ream of almanac-makers, figure-flingers –
    Fellows indeed that only live by stealth,
    Since they do merely lie about stol'n goods –
    They'd make men think the devil were fast and loose,
    With speaking fustian Latin: pray sit down,
    Put on this night-cap sir, 'tis charm'd – and now
    I'll show you by my strong-commanding art
    The circumstance that breaks your duchess' heart.

    A dumb show
    Enter suspiciously, JULIO *and another, they draw a curtain where*
BRACCIANO'S *picture is, they put on spectacles of glass, which*

cover their eyes and noses, and then burn perfumes afore the picture,
and wash the lips of the picture, that done, quenching the fire, and
putting off their spectacles they depart laughing.
Enter ISABELLA *in her nightgown as to bed-ward, with lights after*
her, Count LODOVICO, GIOVANNI, *and others waiting on her, she*
kneels down as to prayers, then draws the curtain of the picture,
does three reverences to it, and kisses it thrice, she faints and will
not suffer them to come near it, dies: sorrow express'd in GIOVANNI
and in Count LODOVICO *she's convey'd out solemnly.*

BRACCIANO   Excellent, then she's dead, –
CONJUROR   She's poisoned,
      By the fum'd picture – 'twas her custom nightly,
      Before she went to bed, to go and visit
      Your picture, and to feed her eyes and lips
      On the dead shadow – Doctor Julio
      Observing this, infects it with an oil
      And other poison'd stuff, which presently
      Did suffocate her spirits.
BRACCIANO   Methought I saw
      Count Lodowick there.
CONJUROR   He was, and by my art
      I find he did most passionately dote
      Upon your duchess – now turn another way,
      And view Camillo's far more politic fate –
      Strike louder music from this charmed ground,
      To yield, as fits the act, a tragic sound.

The second dumb show
Enter FLAMINEO, MARCELLO, CAMILLO, *with four more as Captains,*
they drink healths and dance: a vaulting-horse is brought into the
room: MARCELLO *and two more whisper'd out of the room while*
FLAMINEO *and* CAMILLO *strip themselves into their shirts, as to*
vault: compliment who shall begin: as CAMILLO *is about to vault,*
FLAMINEO *pitcheth him upon his neck, and with the help of the*
rest, writhes his neck about, seems to see if it be broke, and lays
him folded double as 'twere under the horse, makes shows to call
for help: MARCELLO *comes in, laments, sends for the cardinal*
(MONTICELSO) *and Duke* (FRANCISCO), *who comes forth with*
armed men; wonder at the act; FRANCISCO *commands the body*
to be carried home, apprehends FLAMINEO, MARCELLO, *and the*
rest, and (all) go as 'twere to apprehend VITTORIA.

BRACCIANO   'Twas quaintly done, but yet each circumstance
      I taste not fully.
CONJUROR   O 'twas most apparent,

You saw them enter charged with their deep healths
To their boon voyage, and to second that,
Flamineo calls to have a vaulting-horse
Maintain their sport. The virtuous Marcello
Is innocently plotted forth the room,
Whilst your eye saw the rest, and can inform you
The engine of all.
BRACCIANO   It seems Marcello, and Flamineo
Are both committed.
CONJUROR   Yes, you saw them guarded,
And now they are come with purpose to apprehend
Your mistress, fair Vittoria: we are now
Beneath her roof: 'twere fit we instantly
Make out by some back postern –
BRACCIANO   Noble friend,
You bind me ever to you – this shall stand
As the firm seal annexed to my hand.
It shall enforce payment.
CONJUROR   Sir I thank you.

Exit BRACCIANO

Both flowers and weeds spring when the sun is warm,
And great men do great good, or else great harm.

Exit CONJUROR

This scene illustrates several facets of Webster's style and skill as a playwright and poet. It typifies the overall dramatic and theatrical tone of the play with (i) a demonstration, in vivid visual terms, of the machiavellian deceit that takes advantage of such knowledge as Isabella's love for her husband; (ii) the readiness to employ professional assassins who work in devious and deceitful ways, (iii) painful and horrid scenes of death distanced by the use of dumb show, and (iv) brief mimetic interludes, accompanied by music, that are compelling and economical ways of speeding the action towards a subsequent episode, in this case, Vittoria's arraignment. The dumb show was traditionally used as an introduction to a play, (the mime preceding *The Murder of Gonzago* in the play scene of *Hamlet* is, perhaps the best-known example) but Webster uses the device for a different purpose. He presents a complicated series of incidents in an unusually compact and compressed form. The deaths of Isabella and Camillo are essential to the plot and they are accomplished in a theatrically effective manner. Webster daringly uses *two* dumb shows in close proximity but they are striking in their contrasts. Whilst the death of Isabella is sombre, slow-moving and darkly mysterious, Camillo's swift despatch is surrounded by lively, light-hearted action, drinking, dancing and athletic display until the unfortunate 'accident'. Giovanni and Lodovico remain passive, helpless observers in the first scene, but the second dumb show draws the action from theatrical conjuration to a reality which culminates in Vittoria's arrest on suspicion of complicity. The two shows are not really interludes, but unusual means by which the main plot is speedily advanced.

Although seen only briefly, the character of the Conjuror is well drawn. We respond to his denigration of low-class tricksters and the revelation of his superior conjuring skills. These Bracciano admires, and we get yet further insights into the Duke's delight in deceit and subtlety, as well as his callous indifference to his wife's death. 'Excellent, then she's dead' is his abrupt observation. The dumb show reveals the intensity of Isabella's love for her husband. We also identify Lodovico's private passion which becomes of great importance later in the play. The naive Camillo shows no suspicion of Flamineo's duplicity when joining the vaulting competition. This brief scene advances our knowledge of many of the main characters in the play.

Several styles of language are illustrated in the scene. The Conjuror begins with a light, humorous, sarcastic tone. He speaks disdainfully of 'nigromancers' describing a villains' gallery of petty fakers who juggle with cards, make fireworks, parade apparently intelligent horses (curtals), tell fortunes or cast horoscopes. All these would, no doubt, be familiar to Webster's London audience. The Conjuror condemns their 'fustian' Latin. But the mood changes from verbal disparagement to serious conjuration when he moves to the main business of his 'strong commanding' art. Levity gives way to a darker, less comfortable world of black magic. The quick-fire conversation between Bracciano and the Conjuror which follows the mimes rapidly elaborates the details of the murders. Webster shows his skill in devising direct, unambiguous, quick conversation made fluent by the almost overlapping lines as each speaker almost interrupts the former. This exchange contrasts with the extended, descriptive details of the Conjuror's first speech.

The final couplet, spoken by the Conjuror, provides an example of the conventional conclusion to a scene, but it also illustrates Webster's use of *sententiae* – cryptic sayings that offer some moralistic comment on the events that have just been witnessed. The Conjuror observes that great men have power to do good, but simultaneously the ability to cause great harm, in the same way that the warm sun indifferently encourages both flowers and weeds in the garden. This particular maxim was borrowed from a speech in William Alexander's play about Julius Caesar, written in 1607. Its concluding line was 'Great spirits must do great good, or then great ill'. Webster's reworking strengthens the contrast with 'great good' and 'great harm' and focuses our attention on 'men' rather than 'spirits'. His borrowings seldom repeated quotations verbatim. They are used as a basis for a stronger, elaborated more forcefully expressed form of the borrowed phrase or sentence and represent an improvement in meaning, subtlety and poetic shape.

The whole scene also gives a good example of Webster's particular skill in writing verse that compresses meaning and imagery into a particularly economical and concentrated style. In an episode containing only fifty-six lines of verse, in addition to the dumb show, not only do the words rapidly carry forward the plot, but they are couched in muscular verse in which no word is wasted. 'The strong commanding art' immediately transforms the mood from flippancy to seriousness. The precision and vigour of the phrase 'The virtuous Marcello/Is innocently plotted forth the room' succinctly describes the event. With the words 'virtuous' and 'innocent' juxtaposed with 'plotted', Flamineo's deviousness and Marcello's naivety are evoked and contrasted in those three brief words. Such brevity and succinctness can be discovered throughout the play.

PART II: THE DUCHESS OF MALFI

7 SUMMARIES AND

CRITICAL COMMENTARY

THE DUCHESS OF MALFI

Act I, Scene i

Summary

Antonio, steward to the Duchess of Malfi, is welcomed home after a visit to France where he admired the orderly government and absence of corruption. He expresses sympathy for Bosola, returned from a period of imprisonment in the galleys, who seeks to re-establish himself at court. But Bosola receives abrupt treatment from his former employer, the Cardinal, on whose behalf he had committed the murder that led to his prison sentence.

Following a tournament, Ferdinand, Duke of Calabria, and brother to the Cardinal, jokes with his courtiers and learns of Antonio's prowess in jousting. In a private conversation with Delio, a fellow-courtier, Antonio expresses a low opinion of the devious Cardinal and the perversely temperamental Duke. This denigration contrasts strongly with the admiration he shows for the Duchess who is the Duke's twin sister. At Ferdinand's request, she agrees to employ Bosola as her horse steward. In fact, Bosola has been bribed to be a spy in her household. The brothers are determined that the Duchess, a widow, shall not remarry and Bosola is to be their 'intelligencer'.

The Cardinal and Duke, preparing to leave Malfi, firmly warn the Duchess against remarriage. She, however, has a very different intention. Instructing Cariola her maid to be a hidden witness, she invites Antonio into her presence ostensibly to discuss accounts, but, instead, declares her love and desire to have him as her husband. With the exchange of a ring and kisses a secret marriage is solemnised and Antonio is led to the marriage-bed.

Commentary

The principal focus of this opening sequence, divided into three sections, and constituting the whole of Act I, is the secret marriage of the Duchess of Malfi. Her action directly contradicts the express wishes of her two brothers who, for reasons of their own, do not desire to see their sister's remarriage. Whilst Antonio is established as a man of integrity, all the other principal male characters represent shades of villainy and duplicity. Though a church dignitary, the Cardinal is a scheming, devious man, ready to employ law-breaking ruffians to achieve his own ends and rejecting them if they become an embarrassment. The Duke is so obsessively concerned about his sister that he sets Bosola to spy on her. Having learnt the Horse Keeper's past history, we realise that his sinister presence in the Duchess's household represents a serious threat. Her precipitate marriage can do nothing but invite reprimand and reprisal. The Duchess is a woman of considerable spirit as we see from her lively, outspoken ripostes to her brothers' prohibitions. Undoubtedly her love for Antonio is passionate and sincere. But the question is posed – can such a secret marriage survive in such dangerous circumstances?

The scene flows along with considerable speed, introducing characters and developing the plot in a direct, yet subtle, manner. Characters are distinguished by their individual styles of behaviour and speech. Bosola, the coarse, down-to-earth ex-soldier uses rough, often bawdy, prose which he can adapt when talking to his superiors. The courtiers' inconsequential chatter contrasts with the more serious, poetic style employed by Antonio and the fierce image-laden exchanges of the Duchess with her brothers. But she also uses a sensuous, urgent tone in her declaration to Antonio which makes their love-scene vividly dramatic, accompanied as it is with fervent kisses, the presentation of a ring and the revelation of the secret witness, Cariola.

In this first act, the author has created a considerable sense of excitement concerning the outcome of the dangerous course on which the Duchess has embarked. As Cariola remarks, is it a 'spirit of greatness' or 'a fearful madness'?

Act II, Scene i

Summary

Bosola first mocks an elderly gentleman, Castruchio who has misguided ambitions for greatness. He also derides an old woman who has made vain attempts to look younger. That same old woman is a midwife and this strengthens Bosola's impression that the Duchess is expecting a child. He determines to test his theory with a gift of apricots – known to be greatly desired by pregnant women.

Antonio confides to Delio the details of his secret marriage. They then confront Bosola and reprimand him for his assumed melancholy now that he has gained an important position in the Duchess's household. Their badinage is interrupted by the arrival of the Duchess, out of breath, somewhat plump in appearance, short-tempered with her maids but particularly solicitous to Antonio. Having observed the signs of pregnancy, Bosola presents the dish of apricots which the Duchess greedily devours. So his suspicions are confirmed. Unfortunately, the fruit has the effect of precipitating the onset of labour and the Duchess is hurried away by her ladies for the ministrations of the midwife. Antonio is taken aback by the abrupt speed of events. He rejects Delio's suggestion that blame might be attached to Bosola for poisoning the apricots. Such an accusation would attract the attention of the physicians whom they wished to avoid.

Commentary

Bosola's clever deception dominates this scene. We realise that he is an acute observer of the Duchess and her attitude towards Antonio. His apparent deference is only a blind for his distasteful but successful trick with the dung-ripened apricots. In language and imagery he is crude, contemptuous and ironic, whether he is speaking to a courtier, the old woman, Antonio or the Duchess. Indeed he expresses wholesale derision for the nobility, claiming their passions to be as base as those of the meanest citizens.

The scene shows Antonio's great difficulty in responding to his new position. In the barbed exchanges with Bosola, he seems to come off worse. He is easily nonplussed, leaving Delio to make the more positive proposals to handle the emergency. Whilst the Duchess's affection for Antonio is marked in the 'hat' incident which stresses their equality, she is also fearful for their relationship should her pregnancy be discovered. Webster is careful to detail genuine physical symptoms of pregnancy and the 'apricot' test was a well-known means of confirming motherhood.

Act II, Scene ii

Summary

Bosola, certain of the Duchess's condition, rates the old woman midwife with a speech full of sexual innuendo, condemning women as mere creatures of lust. Antonio, now recomposed, orders all exits from the Palace to be barred on the pretext that the Duchess has been robbed and that the criminal must be apprehended before he escapes. Delio is despatched to Rome while Cariola brings Antonio the news that the Duchess has given birth to a son and he immediately sets about having the child's horoscope cast.

Commentary

In his badinage with the midwife and the officers, Bosola continues to exhibit his crude, ironic humour. He is sceptical about Antonio's inventions concerning the theft. With Delio's departure, Antonio is left without a close ally and he is threatened by his deeply suspicious fellow-servant. The birth of the child means that the Duchess's position has become even more hazardous. Difficulties associated with discovery of the marriage and the child begin to overwhelm the delights that the couple have enjoyed.

Act II, Scene iii

Summary

A second confrontation takes place in the garden between a suspicious Bosola and a jumpy Antonio. The Steward explains away the horoscope that he carries as an estimate of the Duchess's losses. He then tries to head off enquiries by accusing Bosola of poisoning the apricots. The imputation is treated with scorn. Antonio suffers a nosebleed (a further symptom of his tension) and the drops of blood blot out his name on the paper. He retreats and in so doing allows the bloodstained paper to fall. Bosola, scooping it up, finds further confirmation of his suspicions about the Duchess. He determines to inform the Duke and the Cardinal, using old Castruchio as a messenger.

Commentary

This scene develops the anxieties of the previous sequence. Antonio finds it difficult to handle emergencies, while Bosola becomes increasingly bold and confident. He laughs off accusations. The device of the dropped horoscope may strain our credulity, but it is an unusual, intriguing method of announcing the birth. Bosola with his very low opinion of morality immediately assumes that Antonio has become the Duchess's 'bawd'. It does not occur to him that the Steward might have become the Duchess's husband. The paper bearing Antonio's blood, telling of threat and violent death, provides a powerful portent of misfortunes to come.

Act II, Scene iv

Summary

The Cardinal engages in a teasing exchange with his mistress, Julia, wife of Castruchio, and formerly Delio's lover. They are interrupted first by a messenger from Malfi and then by Delio who finds Julia very much at home in the Cardinal's lodging. He suspects that the message from Malfi betrays the Duchess and Antonio.

Commentary
Though short, this scene provokes an immediate dramatic development through the transmission of Bosola's suspicions as well as illustrating the lightness of the Cardinal's moral scruples. His attachment to Julia ignores her marriage vows, and reveals him as much a man of the world as Delio. The careless attitude to love and fidelity illustrated in this scene contrasts strongly with the serious, secret, though legally-sanctioned love between Antonio and the Duchess.

Act II, Scene v

Summary
Ferdinand, twin brother to the Duchess, bursts out in furious, obsessive denunciation when he learns of his sister's behaviour. His anger far exceeds that of the Cardinal who counsels caution. Though the Duke rages on with terrible threats of awesome punishments, these passionate outbursts do not lead to any positive action.

Commentary
There is no logical explanation for the Duke's furious outburst with his talk of blasting, infection, coal-pits, pitch and sulphur. True the Duchess has disobeyed his injunction, but she has committed no illegal act. Even if she had, the Cardinal as the spiritual leader ought to appear the more outraged, but he considers his brother's words intemperate. The Duke's obsession with his sister's apparent dishonour and his violent language suggest severe psychological disturbance, even mental unbalance. But we notice that his fury does not provoke immediate retribution. Only when the evidence is unimpeachable will he stir, so that his burning anger is accompanied by a strange feeling of impotence.

The whole scene is shot through with images of destruction – purging, blood-letting, bodily dismemberment, consuming pits of fire and sulphur, each figure more horrific than the last. The language magnifies Ferdinand's seething mental distraction. Since his threats go beyond reason or common sense, they become ominously dangerous.

Act III, Scene i

Summary
When Duke Ferdinand visits his sister in Malfi, he gives no indication that

he is aware of her secret marriage. Instead he discounts any malicious rumours about the Duchess and proposes her marriage to Count Malateste. Later, when alone, he is joined by Bosola bringing news of the three children whose parentage remains uncertain. Ferdinand totally rejects Bosola's suggestion that the Duchess might have been bewitched, insisting that love is subject entirely to human will. Using keys that Bosola has obtained, Ferdinand intends to visit the Duchess's bedroom and find out for himself the exact truth of the matter.

Commentary
Convinced of his sister's deliberate and wilful disobedience, Ferdinand is determined to seek positive proof of her disgrace and of his suspicions of Antonio, using Bosola as an agent. His obsession follows a certain logic, disallowing possible excuses and insisting on personal responsibility. There is also a curious calmness in the Duke's behaviour when he appears to shrug off the suggestions of scandal as insignificant, though his sharp enquiry to Antonio might have been a trick to induce the steward into self-condemning comment.

In terms of chronological time, several years have passed since the end of Act II and in the interim, the Duke seems to have remained quiescent in spite of his threatening accusation. However, in terms of performance, this scene follows the last without any interval so that they are dramatically, if not chronologically, close.

Act III, Scene ii

Summary
There can be no doubt about Antonio and the Duchess's mutual passionate affection. They are seen in intimate embrace, loving and laughing together. A light-hearted trick in which Antonio and Cariola steal out of the room, while the Duchess continues to confess her love, gives Ferdinand the opportunity to emerge from his hiding place and confront her. She shows tremendous courage when Ferdinand urges her to kill herself and assuage the shame. She admits her secret marriage, but resists Ferdinand's vituperative attack on Antonio. With claims that she has defiled the family reputation, the Duke makes an abrupt departure, asserting 'I will never see thee more', thus breaking the family tie. When Antonio returns, the Duchess shows him the dagger presented by the Duke and this conjures up expectations of swift retribution. They are interrupted by knocking and Antonio makes his escape. The newcomer is Bosola reporting the Duke's angry departure from Malfi and the Duchess hurriedly invents the excuse that his annoyance stemmed from her steward's mismanagement of the household accounts.

Bosola is sent to bring officers to arrest Antonio, but before he returns the Duchess instructs her husband to flee for safety to Ancona and there await the arrival of their household goods and valuables. Bosola comes back with the officers to find the Duchess berating Antonio for his poor stewardship and dismissing him from her service. The officers accompanying Bosola enjoy denigrating Antonio, though when they have left Bosola comments sarcastically upon their attitude. He appears to commend Antonio's admirable qualities despite his low birth and in so doing insinuates himself into the Duchess's confidence. She discloses the truth concerning her marriage and the children and entrusts Bosola with the carriage of their coin and jewels to Ancona. Their journey will resemble a pilgrimage.

Commentary

The mood and tone of this scene produce abrupt and dramatic changes. The gentle, teasing behaviour of the opening is rapidly replaced by a confrontation full of threat and physical danger. Until now, the Duke has maintained a certain restraint. He has not admitted knowledge of the marriage, indeed he has actually proposed the elderly Count Malateste as a husband and rebutted any hint of scandal about his sister. Here, in private, having witnessed the lively banter and the passionate kissing, the Duke, frustrated in his own incestuous obsession for his sister, violently denounces the loving couple. Antonio is a lecher, the Duchess is likened to a witch and their love condemned as lust. Yet, despite his rage, Ferdinand remains incapable of real action. All he can do is threaten and denounce. The speed of the scene is maintained after the Duke's departure when we see the quick-thinking Duchess concoct an explanation for her brother's wrath and at the same time plan Antonio's escape. She is very effective in denouncing her steward, but totally deceived by Bosola's apparent sympathy. The feeling of the final sequence is one of considerable irony. Having shrugged off one antagonist, the Duchess accepts another into her deepest confidence.

As the action changes so does the style of language. The loving chatter between Antonio and the Duchess refers to classical love and the three naked goddesses judged by Paris. Then Ferdinand introduces a scathing, derogatory tone, talking of wolves, screech owls, lust, lechery, dogs and monkeys – though his speech does include a brief allegory on reputation. The crude aspersions cast on Antonio by the officers, denouncing him as a Jew, a miser and hermaphrodite are followed by Bosola's contrasting brilliantly ironic comments on the baseness of flatterers and his apparent approbation of Antonio's honesty and excellence as a courtier and faithfulness as a soldier. It is offered with such apparent integrity that the Duchess is entirely persuaded to put her trust in a man whom we know to be a villain. Towards the end of this scene, Bosola's style of speech intro-

duces a verbal felicity not demonstrated before. It has a telling effect on
his persuasive argument and offers a contrast to his usual observations, full
of sexual innuendo and malice – a style to which he returns in the final
soliloquy.

Act III, Scene iii

Summary
The Cardinal and Ferdinand are engaged as soldiers of the Emperor. Delio
and his companion Silvio joke about the lamentable military prowess of
Count Malateste. These critical remarks continue when they are joined by
Bosola. But the news he brings so clearly annoys Ferdinand and the
Cardinal that they seek to secure the banishment of the Duchess and
Antonio from Ancona. The Cardinal's army is to be raised at Loretto –
a stopping-place on the Duchess's journey.

Commentary
Malateste, of whom the soldiers spoke so mockingly, was, of course,
intended as the new husband for the Duchess. In planning their retaliation
against the Duchess, the Cardinal and the Duke demonstrate a cruel
animosity out of all proportion to their sister's alleged error. What prompts
this brotherly outrage? The secret marriage and the unchristened 'beggarly
brats' are an affront to conventional religious practice and thus offensive
to the Cardinal as representative of the church. He is publicly bound to
punish such loose behaviour. Ferdinand's own dark lust for his sister
transforms into an obsession to destroy what he cannot enjoy.

Act III, Scene iv

Summary
The scene which takes place at the Shrine of our Lady of Loretto begins
with two dumb shows. The first presents the Cardinal replacing his spiritual
robes with the weapons of war, followed by a depiction of the banishment
of Antonio, the Duchess and her children from the state of Ancona.
Solemn music and singing accompany the proceedings. Two pilgrim
onlookers offer comment on the precise details of the second mime. The
Pope has provided spiritual authority for the banishment and the Cardinal
angrily wrenches the wedding-ring from the Duchess's finger whilst
threatening revenge.

Commentary
The meeting at the shrine marks the confrontation of the hostile parties.
Now the Duke's threats have become much more serious with the power

of Church and State brought to bear on the Duchess and her husband. Their vulnerable private world is exposed to public view.

Webster introduces a new style of presentation with these dumb shows and ceremonial music. Instead of a realistic confrontation which the preceding events have led us to expect, the effect is heightened by these symbolised actions. Though pomp and ceremony invade the scene, the focus fixes unerringly on the Duchess and her husband. All authority seems to be ranged against them. We are presented with a visual demonstration of the power and scope of their adversaries and the dangers inevitably looming.

Act III, Scene v

Summary
The Duchess and Antonio now find their household much depleted. Servants, sensing impending disaster, have slipped away. Bosola brings a letter from Ferdinand inviting Antonio to Naples, but couched in such ambiguous terms that the apparent sincerity seems to carry a threat to Antonio's life. The Duchess urges her husband to flee to Milan with their eldest son. Shortly after their sorrowful farewell, Bosola returns and orders the Duchess and her remaining children back to her own palace.

Commentary
This is the last time that we shall see the Duchess and her husband alive together and the scene exudes a sense of increasing distress as the servants desert, the ominous letter is received, and the order is given to return as a virtual prisoner. There is some uncertainty in the text as to whether Bosola returns disguised and remains undetected or whether, alternatively, the Duchess, seeing through his disguise, recognises her misplaced trust. By using the fable of the salmon and the dogfish, the Duchess's wretched state is effectively portrayed, but it is also given a certain objectivity through its literary form. She presents an image of her own misery.

Act IV, Scene i

Summary
Ferdinand is frustrated by his sister's stoical acceptance of her imprisonment and determines to disturb her calm with a series of gross mental tortures. At their meeting in a darkened room, although he adopts a tone of reconciliation, the Duke presents her with a dead man's hand bearing the ring that he had earlier torn from the Duchess's hand in the mime scene. Thinking it to be Ferdinand's, she kisses the proffered hand, but discovers when the lamps are relit that it has come from a corpse. Next

she is forced to view a tableau that displays the seemingly dead bodies
of Antonio and her oldest son. All she now desires is death. As she goes
off to pray, the Duke reveals that the bodies are but wax effigies. Even
Bosola seems touched by the Duchess's agony but Ferdinand has not yet
finished his tortures.

Commentary

The physically horrific nature of the tragedy begins to dominate from
this scene onwards. The cruelty is made explicit in the dead hand and
the wax figures. Ferdinand's words of apparent comfort are maliciously
destructive. He shows a total absence of compassion in his obsessive
determination to destroy his sister. On the other hand, Bosola the cynic
expresses pity in his conversations with the Duchess. We may be uncertain
as to how genuine this concern is, but he does urge the Duke to desist
from his cruel practice.

We notice the context in which Webster depicts cruelty and violence.
It is indirectly through tableau or in a darkened room where the effect
is felt rather than seen. Such tableaux afford a very economic method
of handling what might otherwise be complex events. The central intention of causing maximum distress to the Duchess is presented in quick,
vivid, horrifying visions.

Act IV, Scene ii

Summary

With the alleged intention of curing her melancholy, Ferdinand lets loose a
group of distracted madmen into the Duchess's chamber, but their mad
cavortings and wild ravings fail to disturb her. One old man (Bosola in
disguise), remaining after the others have left, creates a chilling atmosphere with his talk of tombs and putrefying flesh. Though they exchange
blackly ironic jokes, her spirit is not broken and she maintains 'I am
Duchess of Malfi still'. The appearance of the executioner with coffin and
rope indicates that the end is clearly close. Cariola is forced out of the
room while Bosola recites a sombre dirge that presages death. The Duchess
submits to strangulation with calm bravery. Her death is swiftly followed
by the murder of Cariola and the Duchess's children. This tableau of
destruction draws expressions of pity from Ferdinand when he enters
to view the bodies, but he finds that he cannot bear the sight of his dead
sister. When the face is again uncovered, the Duke's responses consist
of a garbled mixture of accusation, distraction, self-justification and guilt.
He angrily turns on Bosola accusing him of unjust, bloody murder. Though
vociferous in his defence, Bosola finds himself rejected by the maddened,
distraught Duke. Left alone with the Duchess, Bosola discovers a brief

stirring of life before she finally expires and he speaks a moving elegy over her dead body. Now he recognises his own isolation.

Commentary
Outstanding in this scene is the Duchess's marvellous self-possession. She is not moved to distraction by the lunatics or Bosola's funeral incantations. She faces execution with bravery seeing it as 'the best gift' her brothers can give. Her deepest feelings are given strong sensitive expression:

> Yet I am not mad:
> I am acquainted with sad misery (IV.ii. 26–27).

> Necessity makes me suffer constantly,
> And custom makes it easy (IV.ii. 29–30).

> I am Duchess of Malfi still (IV.ii. 142).

> I know death hath ten thousand doors
> For men to take their exits (IV.ii. 219–20).

> Come violent death
> Serve for mandragora to make me sleep. (IV.ii. 234–5).

She offers stoical acceptance, physical courage and a notable absence of recrimination.

Her attitude and language contrast with the foolish mumblings of the mad and the wild distraction of Ferdinand. Death which she has accepted in calm tones draws from the Duke a frenzied outburst of accusation and self-condemnation. A third style is provided by Bosola's sombre, formal language and his dirge of death. The feelings of pity expressed earlier have not deflected him from his murdering task but after the Duchess's death he expresses remorseful sorrow and finds himself accused by his so-called employer.

The scene switches between violent action and quiet reverie. The murders – the first to be seen in the play – are carried out with calm efficiency. Only Cariola, in contrast with her mistress, struggles with her murderers, attempting futile excuses for survival.

Act V, Scene i

Summary
Ferdinand and the Cardinal intend Antonio to be their next victim. Part

54

of his appropriated property has been given to the Cardinal's mistress, Julia. Delio tries in vain to recover the land through the intervention of the Marquis of Pescara, but he is unwilling to conduct transactions in property so unjustly gained. The Marquis also gives news of Ferdinand's strange illness. Unaware of his wife's death, Antonio determines to confront the Cardinal hoping to achieve a reconciliation.

Commentary
The irony of the scene lies in Antonio's ignorance. All attempts at intercession will be doomed to failure because we know the fearful animosity of his antagonists. Ferdinand's sickness is first described as apoplexy or frenzy – illnesses often induced by melancholy or madness. His earlier obsessive behaviour has developed into a kind of insanity.

Act V, Scene ii

Summary
Ferdinand's condition is now identified by a doctor as lycanthropy, a disease in which the patient imagines himself to be a wolf. When he appears, the Duke behaves strangely, trying to throttle his own shadow. He is humoured with tricks but they have little effect. The Cardinal, having watched this episode, seeks to find some excuse for his brother's antics, blaming it on the appearance of an apparition. When interrupted by Bosola, the Cardinal feigns ignorance of his sister's death. He abruptly dismisses Julia's invitation to supper. She, meantime, has noticed the physical attractiveness of Bosola. The Cardinal leaves, having given instructions for the murder of Antonio with Delio used as a pawn. Julia returns to confess her passion for Bosola and both engage in amorous word-play. He persuades her to seek the cause of the Cardinal's melancholy.

Responding to Bosola's request, Julia applies her blandishments. Having tired of her presence, the Cardinal at first resists, but finally blurts out the truth of the murder to the horrified woman. She is sworn to secrecy on a poisoned Bible and she dies moments later as Bosola emerges from hiding, having overheard the Cardinal's admission. They exchange blunt accusations and the Cardinal alternatively threatens and cajoles Bosola who is wary of further risky demands on his services. Eventually he agrees to undertake the murder of Antonio, but in a closing soliloquy admits his intention of saving the Duchess's husband as a penitential act for her murder.

Commentary
The whole scene alternates between sequences of noisy raving and murder and playful amorous exchanges apparently belonging to a different world.

Bosola's final soliloquy is full of regret. A sense of general mistrust pervades the scene. All the conversation is tinged with madness, suspicion or wariness as each character acts according to his own self-interest. Ferdinand's raving represents a perpetual threat of disclosure, Julia smarts under her rejection. The Cardinal jealously guards then foolishly reveals his secret, instantly regretting the decision by killing his confidante. Bosola responds so sharply that his words carry no guarantee that the Cardinal's orders will be carried out. We have yet to see if Bosola's acts correspond with expressed intentions.

The atmosphere of increasing horror is created by the Duke's wild talk of churchyards, dead bodies and hacked limbs. Love-talk is followed by murder. The quarrel between the Cardinal and Bosola is full of destruction, hewing to pieces, rotten purposes, dirty tricks and blood-letting. The final speech paints a vivid picture of the 'slippery ice-pavement' on which men intent on destruction must tread.

Act V, Scene iii

Summary

Antonio and Delio approach the Cardinal's lodgings, pausing in nearby ruins where an echo (from the Duchess's grave) warns of the dangers that confront them. Antonio expresses his determination to continue.

Commentary

Webster makes skilful use of the ghostly echo. The carefully worded speeches each have a concluding phrase that when repeated add up to a powerful injunction to flee.

Act V, Scene iv

Summary

The Cardinal gives orders for the Duke to be left in isolation. He and his brother are not to be disturbed for any reason whatsoever. The instruction is intended to facilitate the removal of Julia's body with the help of Bosola whom he intends to kill immediately afterwards – a plan which Bosola overhears. First a distracted Ferdinand passes through the chamber and then Antonio, who is mistakenly stabbed by Bosola believing him to be an adversary. As Antonio dies he learns of the death of his wife and two younger children.

Commentary

Threats of death now begin to assume a terrible physical reality. We notice each murder occurs through error or wildness rather than in calculated assassination. The first victim is the innocent Antonio whose only fault was a secret marriage. His final agony is to hear of his wife's death. The Cardinal's carefully-laid plans for the murder of Bosola and the disposal of Julia's corpse are to rebound on him. Throughout the scene, Webster maintains a sense of uncertainty and fear even though the deaths are obviously imminent. Nothing happens precisely as planned.

Act V, Scene v

Summary
Bosola brings the body of Antonio to the Cardinal and threatens to kill him. Cries for assistance go unregarded by the courtiers ordered to stay away. As Bosola stabs repeatedly at the priest, the maddened Ferdinand joins the fray, lunging wildly at both men, but the Duke receives a death-wound from Bosola who is now certain that he has accomplished revenge for the Duchess, Antonio and Julia. However this triumph is shortlived. He too receives a fatal wound as the courtiers break into the chamber. Last to enter is Delio bringing Antonio's eldest son, the sole survivor of the Malfi household.

Commentary
This ugly animal-like struggle among the three men, one madly stabbing at his brother, the other calling vainly for aid and the third desperate to complete his task of revenge provides a horrific climax to the play. Of the cool, self-composed brothers who issued such stern commands to the Duchess at the opening of the play, one is driven mad, the other caught in the toils of his own treachery. Bosola, who initially seemed harshly insensitive, proves to possess some feelings of pity and concern. But death is the common outcome for all. Their dying words comment aptly on their realisation of human folly with no expectation of forgiveness or hope.

> O, this gloomy world.
> In what a shadow, or deep pit of darkness,
> Doth womanish and fearful mankind live! (V. v. 100-3)

The entrance of the young prince offers a brief upsurge of hope. The Duchess's death which preceded the horrible conclusion demonstrates a braveness, patience and courage unique to her. Her positiveness in death offers a shining contrast to the sordid murders with which the play concludes.

8 THEMES

8.1 ENDURANCE: SUSTAINED LOVE IN ADVERSITY

The Duchess's remarriage provides the central conflict of the tragedy yet no legal objection can be raised against her action. As a widow she is free to marry again, and the ceremony, if somewhat unorthodox, is perfectly valid. The unequal status of the partners leads the Duchess to propose a secret marriage, a foolish, but not an illegal, decision. The Duchess cannot be condemned for any outrageous legal or spiritual misconduct. Indeed what shines through all the surrounding hostility is a powerful sense of a woman's passion for the man whom she loves, not because of his position or wealth, but solely for his own personal qualities. That love is unwaveringly steadfast despite trials that would challenge the composure and sensibility of the bravest of women.

Bosola, the planted spy, is her first adversary. Encouraged by the trick pregnancy test and the purloined horoscope, he betrays her motherhood, even though he does not identify the father. The Duchess is then forced to face furious denunciations from her brother, followed by chilling encounters with the dead man's hand, the deceptive images of her lifeless husband and children and the incursion of madmen. Even when confronted by the executioners with their coffin and ropes, she exhibits a marvellous calm dignity. Throughout the play the devotion of the Duchess remains constant. Her passionate ardour for Antonio is no passing infatuation for a young, attractive servant, but deep, sincere and lasting. Never, throughout all the tribulations does she utter one hint suggesting a wish for an alternative, less dangerous course. On the contrary, in each horrific incident, the Duchess reiterates a readiness to endure all privations: 'I am arm'd against misery' (III.v. 142). Bosola remarks on her

> behaviour so noble
> As gives a majesty to adversity (IV. i. 5-6)

'I am Duchess of Malfi still' (IV.ii. 142) she asserts after a visit from the madmen and Bosola's torturing words. Her final speech is unfrightened and dignified. Love sustained in adversity is a theme that emerges strongly from the play. It is particularly contained in the enduring love which the Duchess shows for Antonio and her children, a devotion which upholds her in the face of the most frightful and undeserved antagonism.

8.2 AN EXPLORATION OF MARRIAGE

There is no doubt that the Duchess's marriage is at the heart of the play. Clifford Leech (*Webster: The Duchess of Malfi*) points out three of its hazards – inequality, secrecy and the fact that it is a second marriage. We also know that it is directly contradictory to the expressed wishes of her brothers. In making this marriage a central theme of the play, Webster sets the conventional, orthodox and legal against the unconventional and unorthodox without suggesting any illegality. The couple are within the bounds of law but outside normal conventions. For this they suffer death, innocent of any grievous sin. Such injustice contributes powerfully to the whole mood of the play.

The Duchess and Antonio are undoubtedly deeply in love with each other. We quickly learn of his admiration for her and she swiftly demonstrates her passion with a proposal of marriage. This is no sordid affair such as the Cardinal's liaison with Julia, but genuine, honest and consummated in marriage. Admirable though he may be, Antonio is clearly of lower social status than the Duchess and she is flouting convention in this unequal partnership. As the pilgrims observe at the Loretto shrine:

> who would have thought
> So great a lady would have matched herself
> Unto so mean a person. (III.iv. 24-6).

The meanness cannot refer to Antonio's character but to his social status. Whilst Jacobean audiences may have joined in that condemnation, contemporary readers feel more than a little sympathy for the couple suffering from class prejudice.

The second element, its secrecy, relates to two issues: the legitimacy of a marriage conducted in such privacy and the effect of withholding the information from the brothers. A secret ceremony in which the couple exchange vows before a witness – *per verba de presenti* – does constitute a legal marriage. The Duchess sees little need for any futher religious elaboration, but the arrangement is hedged about with a number of reservations. For example, consummation of such a marriage should be delayed until confirmed by a religious ceremony. This is certainly not the case with the Duchess who immediately invites Antonio into her bed and, in due course, produces several children who remain unbaptised. The secret marriage is seen as an act of defiance against the accepted orthodoxy of the church. The reasons for the brothers' prohibition are only sketchily outlined. The Duke and the Cardinal proclaim their general antipathy towards the marriage of widows, suggesting that such unions mean loss of virtue and giving way to baser instincts. But none of these arguments, including the Duke's about maintaining family property, seems particularly persuasive. The antipathy remains unexplained until the Duke's own secret feelings towards his sister are exposed.

In summarising the marriage theme, we find a story of two people, one a steward, the other a widowed Duchess, falling in love, getting married in secret and begetting children. These events produce most tragic consequences. All but one of the family die but not before the Duke, most vociferous in his opposition, is driven mad. Prejudice, private obsession and narrow orthodoxy combine to shatter the glorious dreamworld of the secret marriage.

8.3 BLOOD AND LUST

A critic, Robert Hewison, noted in a recent production of *The Duchess of Malfi*, an emphasis which he described as 'blood and lust, indeed lust after someone of one's own blood' (*Sunday Times*, 2 July 1985). This stark appraisal of the play is confirmed by Ferdinand's dying couplet:

> Whether we fall by Ambition, blood or lust.
> Like diamonds we are cut with our own dust. (V.v. 72-3)

Stirred blood releases intense emotion which issues in love or lust. In each case it is self-destructive. Antonio senses fire in the Duchess's blood when she declares her love for him. Cariola sees that stirring as a fearful madness. Indeed the outcome is strangulation for the Duchess and an accidental, bloody death for Antonio. The Cardinal's lust is satisfied by his mistress Julia, but his cooling desire and her sudden passion for Bosola's 'lively sparks of roughness' lead to her poisoning and the Cardinal's death when he attempts to cover up the murder by disposing of the body. These outward shows of lust are contrasted by the inward tortured, raging desire of Ferdinand. When he learns of the Duchess's child, his violent response is couched in terrifying burning images. 'We must not now use balsmum [a balm] but fire' to cleanse the infection. He would have the bodies cremated in pitch and sulphur, the child boiled in a stew. He talks of stinging whips and scorpions. His mind and body seem to be on fire with lust. In a maddened outburst of disgust, Ferdinand describes his sister's heart as a

> hollow bullet
> Filled with unquenchable wild-fire (III.ii. 115-16)

Perhaps it more accurately describes his own tortured state of mind which soon turns to obsessive cruelty, resulting in a broken body and demented lycanthropic delusion. The Duke, the Cardinal and the Duchess are close blood relations. Burning desire or hot lust draws them all to the 'everlasting cold' of death.

8.4 DECEIT

The majority of the leading characters are essentially deceitful. Driven by desire for advancement, ambition or lust, they employ undercover and at times, machiavellian schemes. But in no case do their ploys bring or maintain security. Despite their over-confident self assurance all are outwitted or destroyed. Bosola, the Duke and the Cardinal all carry unsuspected, self-destructive charges. Webster does not invite us to admire or vicariously to enjoy the cunning deceptions whether by dung-ripened apricots, dead hands, wax corpses or poisoned Bibles. Rather do we revolt against this inexcusably cruel behaviour. A strong moral judgement on deception is implied in the punishments visited upon the schemers. Rather than suffer any legal or spiritual reprimand, they inflict self-imposed penalties. The irony is that the innocent deceptions of the Duchess and Antonio also bring down wrath and unjustified punishment.

9 INTERPRETATIONS

9.1 SENSATIONALIST THEATRE

If all the sensational events are lumped together, it is easy to condemn the play as a sordid chamber of horrors inhabited by flocks of madmen, wax figures, corpses, coffins and hangmen's ropes with a final obliterating shoot-out providing a suitably theatrical climax. But we must be wary of regarding the play as mere vicarious sensationalism. This need becomes more apparent when we look at the pattern of events. First there is a marriage proposal, then a secret wedding and the birth of a baby. Whilst the brothers are angry, they make no immediate attempt to slaughter the innocent. Indeed years pass. When the Duke's fury is voiced, the Cardinal urges caution. Their language may become violent, but there is no deliberately cruel physical act until the point when the Duchess and Antonio are banished from Ancona. This abuse, however, is presented mimetically with the Duchess's ring being dragged from her finger. Only in Act IV does the Duke's accelerated mental obsession gain such momentum that cruelty becomes explicit with the hand, the wax figures and the procession of madmen. So far no blood has been shed. Once gained, the intensity never slackens and the destruction of the Duchess, so long expected, finally takes place. Only then is violence unleashed when illogic, misunderstanding and deceit commingle, and destruction ensues. All this is contained in a comparatively brief section of the play and is rapidly over. Though Webster creates a pattern that instigates a threat, becomes increasingly ominous and finally breaks out in violence, the destructive phases are interspersed with quiet scenes of reflection, loving exchanges and calm bravery. We can discern a carefully modulated drama that develops maximum excitement when events reach their inevitable conclusion and not just a miscellaneous collection of horrific episodes.

In *History of the Theatre* (Boston: Allyn & Bacon, 1968) Oscar Brockett observes two trends in Jacobean tragedy:

The preoccupation with penetrating questions about man's nature and achievement abated in favour of interesting stories told for their own sakes. Thrills and excitement began to take precedence over significant insights or complex characterisation... At the same time technical skill increased. The playwrights handled expositions more adroitly, compressed the action into fewer episodes, built complications to startling climaxes and alternated quiet with tumultuous scenes (p.167).

Webster's play is a good example of this trend. The sensational story coming from Italy, infamous for its decadence and immorality, is coupled with machiavellian cynicism and villainy and the actual staging is influenced by the ancient plays of the Roman Seneca who delighted in blood and death in theatrical entertainment.

9.2 PERCEPTIVE CONCERN FOR THE CHARACTERS AND SOCIETY PORTRAYED

The world of the Duchess of Malfi includes the powerful and important. Together, her brothers the Duke and the Cardinal represent the principal temporal and spiritual influences in that society so that their actions have public as well as private consequences. They are served by a group of courtiers, the majority of whom sycophantically ape their masters' views and responses. Some are vain and misguided like Castruchio. Others, like the Marquis of Pescara, exhibit some integrity. In breeding and position, the widowed Duchess is by no means inferior to her brothers. Her marriage to the Duke of Malfi has ensured the continuation of her elevated position. So we see constituted a tightly-knit, exclusive society, sure and certain of its own status. Into this group enter two characters; Antonio having, and Bosola seeking, a position in the Duchess's household. Though we know nothing to Antonio's detriment (indeed he is introduced as virtuous, thoughtful, observant and athletically skilled) he certainly holds an inferior position in the social hierarchy. So too, does Bosola, an altogether rougher, life-hardened character. The more passive Antonio is quickly elevated, but finds himself uncomfortable in his new position, despite the loving concern of his new wife. He experiences difficulty in taking command, shows little political strategy and is no match for Bosola when he is recognised as an adversary. In contrast, Bosola is quick to take advantage of his new post – ever alert, at work for his masters but finding an unexpected challenge to his initial estimate of the Duchess's personality and behaviour.

Her goodness provokes feelings that he had not anticipated and, though her murderer, he becomes her advocate.

Webster cleverly explores the implications of fractured class barriers and our sympathies move with the individuals as they confront their difficulties. Bosola's rejection by the Cardinal seems a harsh rebuff especially considering the pain he has suffered. Antonio obviously admires the Duchess. His shyness and reluctance to respond to this intimacy is effectively portrayed. Her actions demonstrably break the conventions and expose her lively, bold personality, willing to challenge the accepted hierarchical structure of the society. A kind of descant to her unconventional, passionate love for Antonio is provided by the Cardinal and Julia (ex-lover of Delio and wife to Castruchio). Within the class, deviation is apparently condoned. The duchess's unpardonable error is to break out of her class and take a husband of inferior status. This is what provokes the brothers' animosity.

It is perfectly possible to understand the play as having a concern to recognise those individuals who become victims of a particular system because their behaviour fails to conform with accepted norms. The unhappy clash of convention and class with individual desire and personal status is not unknown in our own contemporary society.

9.3 A SENSE OF REALITY

Although the plot of *The Duchess of Malfi* is derived principally from William Painter's *Palace of Pleasure* (1567), Muriel Bradbrook (*John Webster: Citizen and Dramatist*) gives a detailed and lengthy account of several contemporary scandals in Jacobean London that are relevant to the play. She tells of the notorious adventures of a Spaniard, Antonio Perez, whose spying activities not only permeated the Spanish Court and included the denunciation of the Princess of Eboli, but also engaged in intrigues in London, involving many of the English nobility. Professor Bradbrook draws comparisons between the Perez story and *The Duchess of Malfi*, particularly in the episodes of imprisonment when the Princess, like the Duchess, showed great resilience. In his espionage and counter-espionage, Antonio Perez offered a good model for Bosola and the ducal deceits and machinations. However horrific and mind-challenging the events of the play may be, there were sufficient contemporary instances to give them an uncomfortable reality. Evidence was close at hand in London to prevent the events in the play being dismissed as foreign sensationalism.

9.4 RELATIONSHIP TO TRAGEDY

Both Antonio and the Duchess suffer tragic fates, one mistakenly stabbed, the other dying with heroic patience. The play has much in common with many Jacobean tragedies that conclude in the deaths of the chief protagonists. Yet Webster seems to create a special case for Antonio and the Duchess. Although their marriage proves to have such tragic consequences, it cannot really be described as resulting from a tragic error. In discussing the marriage, words like unorthodox, contrary to convention have been used, but in no sense was it illegal or especially sinful. Antonio's defects of personality and the Duchess's over-adventurousness cannot be considered as truly tragic flaws. Irving Ribner refers to the impact of 'human integrity and the nobility to which human life can aspire in spite of the disorder which surrounds it' (*Jacobean Tragedy: The Quest for Moral Order*). Ribner believes the play to be a study of enduring nobility in the face of injustice and suffering. There is little to condemn in the Duchess, even if we have slight concern for what might be minor faults. Instead we trace the story of a woman of considerable bravery, adventurous, resolute, risk-taking, resisting vindictive retribution. Though beset by unrecognised adversaries, she declares and consummates her love for Antonio. They delight in each other and their children. When the process of retribution commences, she shows strength of mind and, in Act IV when death approaches, remarkable resilience to odious tortures. Her patience, steadfastness and bravery in the face of such intense and concentrated evil exhibits human dignity rising above degradation. There can be no escape from her fate. Her brothers are obvious enemies and Bosola, whom she inadvertently trusts, their agent. She voices no recrimination, no accusation of treachery, neither does she cringe or cry for mercy. Ferdinand is intent on inducing despair, but he is unsuccessful. In death she dazzles, bringing about in Bosola a change that she could not effect in life. Antonio, seeking reconciliation with those whom we know to be immutable, meets his death bravely. He rejects advice for safety from Delio, showing 'contempt for pain.'

The Duchess is not, therefore, a tragic heroine suffering because of some fatal flaw in her character, but an exemplar for endurance against injustice and suffering. The endurance is not simply piteous or submissive, but strong, defiant and dignified. This noble stance assigns a value to sustained human dignity, highlighted by the surrounding chaos of cynicism, selfishness and cruelty.

9.5 CONFLICT BETWEEN DESTRUCTION AND CREATION

'A conflict between the two primal forces in the universe, the powers of destruction and the power that nourishes life' is how Alvin Kernan describes the play in his essay on Webster (*Revels History of Drama in English*, III (London, 1975) p.399). The overwhelming impression of the agencies opposing the Duchess is of their destructiveness. Neither the Duke nor the Cardinal ever makes a life-enhancing move. They are always concerned with restriction, prohibition, punishment, gratuitous cruelty. No gesture towards their sister is ever warm, considerate or positive. Her function in the family is as an object to be manipulated for their purposes. What dominates is their readiness to reject, or discard, to use men and women as instruments for their own wiles, regardless of any moral implications. As leaders of State and Church, they display total selfishness, valuing no one but themselves. This negative attitude is further enforced by Bosola, disgruntled, abused, a willing agent of destruction who murders the Duchess and Antonio and supervises the deaths of Cariola and the children. Though he may experience feelings of compassion and a change of heart, the harsh truth is that he is a hired killer who efficiently completes his allotted task. His attitude to the world is cynical and corrosive. This negative tone is also displayed in a particularly horrific manner in the scene with the madmen. The disjunction of life is manifested by the lunatic lawyers, priests and doctors who would normally be associated with health, order and piety. They demonstrate the mental breakdown of humanity and Bosola in the guise of the tomb-maker and executioner personifies this gloomy, negative view of the world and the fragility of human life and reason.

In the Duchess and Antonio an entirely opposite mood is created. From their relationship, we gain a sense of joy and delight in love, marriage and child-rearing. The wooing scene is delicate, sensual. We enjoy the feminine skill with which the Duchess encourages Antonio, his tentativeness, her warm responsiveness. The woman is alive with feelings, leaving the mourning widow behind. The mutual attraction is not to become a casual affair, but a genuine husband-and-wife relationship (in complete contrast to the Castruchio–Cardinal–Julia liaison)' Webster accurately and delicately displays the character of the pregnant woman. The Duchess is slightly tetchy with her maids, but tender to her husband. They delight in the birth of the child despite the attendant dangers. The bedroom embraces, the association of marriage with the fruitfulness of nature, the erotic images of naked goddesses and the teasing love-talk combine to create an idyll of sensual joy and fertility, of affection as a power 'that nourishes life'. Irving Ribner reminds us that the Duchess's speeches 'are full of references to nature: fruit, birds, trees, the heavens, symbols of life and continuity' whereas 'destructive, predatory animals' provide the images for the Duke and the Cardinal – bloodhounds, vipers, a tiger, crows, magpies and caterpillars. (R. V. Holdsworth (ed.), *Webster: The White Devil and The Duchess of Malfi* (London, 1984) pp. 138-9). The contrasts between the creative and destructive images underline the opposition between the powers that nourish life and the powers of destruction.

10 TECHNICAL FEATURES

10.1 PLOT AND STRUCTURE

The full text of William Painter's *Palace of Pleasure* which was Webster's immediate source can be found in an appendix of Leech and Craik's *Revels History of Drama*. Painter's version was taken from the French *Histoires Tragiques* by Belleforest. He had considerably expanded the original story written by the Italian, Matteo Bandello, who actually knew the real Duchess of the title. It is possible to trace in detail the emendations and alterations that Webster makes to Painter's, Belleforest's and Bandello's versions, but essentially the play is his response to those earlier texts rather than a dramatisation of them. The play falls into two main sections: 'the secret marriage' and 'the Duke's revenge'. Our interest in this two-part plot does not lie in following an orderly sequence of events but in moments when characters challenge orthodoxy and then experience the ferocity of cruel, unjustifiable revenge.

The first acquaintance with Antonio and the Duchess and their subsequent wooing engages our sympathy and admiration for the romantic energy of the Duchess who defies her brothers' unreasonable commands and wins herself a husband. The secrecy gives a special piquancy to the plot (as does the secret marriage in *Romeo and Juliet*), but the sense of joy is severely modified by the presence of Bosola, placed in the Duchess's household by the brothers. Bosola's crude evaluation of all sexuality means that he degrades such love as that of the Duchess and Antonio. Clearly no sympathy can be expected from that quarter. The risk attending the unequal, secret marriage is compounded by the birth of the child. It raises questions of legitimacy and fatherhood and also provides positive proof of disobedience. The tension of the first part of the play exists in this risk of discovery. The wily Bosola amply displays his skill as an adversary with the trick of the apricots, his ability to disconcert Antonio and by snatching up the dropped horoscope. His report to the Duke and the Cardinal in Rome sets the second half of the story in motion.

Labelling the second section 'the Duke's revenge' is not an entirely accurate description. Revenge normally implies retribution for some significant evil perpetrated on the revenger, but we cannot describe the secret marriage as a wicked act committed against the Duke. The force and horror of the second part lies in exposing the selfishly vicious nature and motives of the Duchess's adversaries. The Cardinal is portrayed as a man given to fleshly lust, having scant regard for the proprieties of marriage. His mistress, Julia, is installed in his palace. His outrage at the news of the baby in no way matches that of his brother. Indeed he tries to calm Ferdinand's outbursts. He plays little part in the revenge process until he becomes alarmed at his brother's increasing insanity. In taking pains to preserve him, he actually precipitates the Duke's death. The Cardinal is little more than an accessory. The Duke is the prime mover. His responses provide the substance of this part of the play.

The deep sense of physical disgust contained in his outpourings suggests some terrible internal perversion despite the excuses about family honour and fortunes. It is the threat contained in his raging that provides the tension. Then threat is replaced by action – banishment, arrest, imprisonment, torment and torture ending in the Duchess's strangulation. This series of increasingly distressing events cannot be explained in rational terms. They far outweigh the nature of the alleged misdemeanour. But they are entirely logical only as machinations of a madman's mind seeking to destroy his victim.

Finally the horrors of torture are replaced by an orgy of killing. Murder, intended or accidental is apparently the only remedy. The Duke's revenge concludes in the death of himself, his brother, the spy Bosola and Julia. The dignified death of the Duchess stands out in vivid contrast to that final sordid heap of bodies. Such is the outcome of a madman's revenge.

Although the parts have been discussed separately, it does not mean that there is a lack of continuity. This is maintained by the characters who remain active in both parts even though the focus and balance is changed. Essentially the plot consists of the responses of characters to the initial prohibition. All that subsequently happens derives from that source.

Structure

The play is divided into the customary five acts and Professor Bradbrook provides convenient labels for each act:– The Court; The Bedchamber; The World; The Prison; The Graveside. This particular pattern of scenes provides a sense of continuity and identifies the particular focus and emphasis of each act.

Act I centres on 'The Court' and the events leading to the marriage. But it also gives insights into the corrupt nature of that Court through

Antonio's comparisons with France. The villainy of the Duke and the Cardinal is described by the aggrieved Bosola and the straightforward Antonio. Speech after speech refers to betrayal, covetousness, devilish possession, crude jests, deceit, bribery and lust. These distasteful revelations create a menacing atmosphere of corruption and suspicion that bodes ill for the Duchess.

From the public Court we move to the private 'Bedchamber'. The birth of a child is a natural consequence of marriage, but the delight of this event is soured by Bosola's apricot-trick and the Duke's gruesome response. The secret pleasures of the bedchamber, the joys of marriage and motherhood are darkened by treachery and threat.

The third act, 'The World', shows the development of that threat. The brief idyll is soon disturbed. After the angry outburst, the Duke returns to Rome, Antonio, now in public disgrace, prepares to flee to Ancona where the Duchess is to follow him. Their route via the Shrine of our Lady of Loretto brings a confrontation with their adversaries. The action has moved out of Malfi and the scene has been enlarged with a series of damaging episodes, ill-timed flight, arrests, banishment and isolation. The events are now public, exposed to the world. The scale of the opposition is daunting. The great military mime and denunciation shows the Duchess and Antonio pitted against the secular and religious powers of State and Church. The Cardinal, invoking Papal authority seizes the Duchess's possessions and the Duke symbolically wrenches off the wedding ring. The splendid ritual, accompanied by solemn music and singing lifts the denunciation from the realistic to the theatrically symbolic. The couple are condemned before the world.

Act IV, 'The Prison', shows the Duchess undergoing a ritualistic trial by ordeal with the dead-man's hand, the waxworks and the torment of madmen. All the personal qualities of the Duchess are displayed in her resistance to these stylised tortures. The audience now views a dark interior in which the Duchess's qualities shine like a beacon. Even in her death she 'dazzles'. Her defiance in the prison sequence is symbolised by her calm resistance to the chamber of horrors.

Act V which Professor Bradbrook called 'The Graveside' shows the universality of death which draws no distinctions between the just and the unjust. One by one in bloody error, the protagonists are killed. Claims of revenge ring hollowly over the strewn corpses of the Duke, the Cardinal, Bosola and Antonio with the Duchess, Cariola and the children already dead. This Act shows the condition of a world in chaos, where selfishness, ambition and deceit breed conflict in which the guilty and innocent suffer alike. It is prevented from being entirely pessimistic by the unfolding revelation of the quality of the Duchess's character in the face of undeserved, cruel adversity. Act V might be considered an unnecessary aftermath, but it is vital in completing the total picture which shows the Duchess's actions in relation to the world in which she lives. Her life represents a progress from the pomp and ceremony of court through the pleasures of love and the hazards of the world to the final inevitability of the grave.

10.2 CHARACTERISATION

The Duchess

Discussion of the plot and themes of the play have already established the central position that the Duchess holds in the drama. In considering her character, we shall focus on the particular nature of her status in society and the decisive steps she takes to challenge the structure of that society. She belongs to a family familiar with power and authority. Her brothers represent secular and ecclesiastical government. As widow of the Duke of Malfi she has become responsible for managing a large estate and a whole retinue of retainers. From the start we notice how much her personality differs from those of her malicious and devious brothers. They try to pressure her into remaining a widow, by intemperate, threatening, coarse language, but she is by no means subdued. Immediately after their departure she shows mettle and passion in the courtship of Antonio. Her forthright approach, though delicately couched, discloses a woman capable of deep feeling, ready to defy opposition. We are impressed by her assurance and persistence. As a woman in a man's world, she makes a bold, sympathetic impression, but her married state makes her a more vulnerable target especially with a spy in the household. In his vivid portrait of the pregnant Duchess, Webster neatly captures the whims and food-fads as well as the physical condition of motherhood. The sensual, feminine nature of the Duchess's character is not stifled by her brothers' injunctions, but with them, her tone is brisk and uncompromising. In the confrontation she displays a lively intelligence, quick to devise excuses for Antonio's departure. Her error, under pressure, is to misread the devious Bosola's attitude and place a misguided trust in him. That single misjudgement has serious consequences.

The imprisonment demonstrates another facet of the Duchess's character – her indomitable spirit. The physically-vile tricks and traps that Ferdinand sets fail to distract her. She is required to kiss the hand of a corpse, view the dead bodies of her husband and children, suffer an invasion of hideous, dancing, chanting lunatics, confront the instruments of death. Nothing affects her. Her steadfast calm in adversity can excite nothing but admiration. Each new sequence of the play develops and deepens the Duchess's character. Her positive qualities are undeniable yet critics have observed 'marriage to a man unworthy of her is a disastrous mistake' or 'the Duchess, by failing to publish her marriage, destroys her own good name'. Another condemns 'her neglect of rule and jesting with religion, her base, secret and second marriage'. These negative comments may have some technical justification, but Webster seems intent on creating a character of some depth and complexity with recognisable human contradictions rather than a stereotype virtuous widow who dies for love. Her unorthodox, unconventional, but not wicked, behaviour is exposed to a world of corrupt social, moral and religious judgement. Our sympathies must be with her.

Bosola

What is striking about the Duchess's adversaries is their variety and individuality. Webster has created a group who, though united against her (at least initially), display very distinctive responses and attitudes that can constantly surprise and shock. Perhaps the most complex is Bosola. His responsibility for, or supervision of, so many deaths seems to classify him as a bloodthirsty blackguard with few redeeming features. Certainly he spies on the Duchess, deceiving her in action and words. His sombre torments in the guise of tomb-maker end in the Duchess's strangulation. No pity is demonstrated to his victims. Yet this intense cruelty effects a significant change in Bosola leading him to seek retribution for the murder he himself committed. The hard case is cracked; his bitter cynical disregard of life is challenged by the example of the Duchess. Initially Bosola is a character for whom we may feel some sympathy. The Cardinal has used him as an instrument and shows great reluctance to recompense him for his suffering. Our sympathy evaporates when he displays his coarseness and cunning as an 'intelligencer', asserting a conscious cynicism that betrayal will gain reward. Having established such an image of evil, we find a reluctance to respond to his change of heart. Whether it is sincere or not, his description of the imprisoned Duchess paints a telling portrait in language far removed from his earlier coarser style. We detect a change of tone in his words that may prefigure a change of heart. He actually says 'Now, by my life, I pity you', and 'Look you, the stars shine still'. These are expressions of compassion and hope. He urges Ferdinand to desist from his cruelty. We find, however, that Bosola's attempts at recompense prove puny. Webster does not allow conversion to right the wrongs. The final acts are as full of horror as the deliberately murderous acts performed earlier. Robert Ornstein summarises Bosola as:

> a malcontent, embittered by experience and hungry for security which advancement will afford. . . He is capable of true moral feelings [and] finally appalled by Ferdinand's insane revenge. . . Despite

his newfound moral courage, however, Bosola never escapes from the mist of error that enshrouds his life (*The Moral Vision of Jacobean Tragedy*, 1960, 143-4).

Duke Ferdinand

Ferdinand, Duke of Calabria, is an intriguing and complex character. As twin to the Duchess he is physically and emotionally close. His attachment takes an unexpected and dubious form. His excuse for prohibiting the Duchess's remarriage is its detrimental effect on the family fortunes, but his instructions to her are accompanied by an underlying physical threat with 'my father's poniard'. Ferdinand, ready to joke with his courtiers, is quick to reprimand any undue levity. Antonio refers to his 'perverse and turbulent nature'. Sarcastic derision is his favourite amusement. The Duke is a character whose inner world lacks consistency with his outward appearance. The intensity of his reprimand to the courtiers, his unsympathetic tone with the Duchess suggest an inner turbulence that could prove dangerous. This is coupled with a machiavellian deceitfulness in planting a spy in his sister's household. Then an eruption takes place. All that compressed tension bursts out in a furious tirade against his sister when he learns of the child. His language is extreme. The Duchess is a 'notorious strumpet', she has employed a bawd to sate her lust and he cries for her utter destruction. What motivates this intemperate, excessive rage? The alleged lapse is exactly what Ferdinand warned the Duchess against in the first scene, but there is little rationality in his outburst. It is motivated by some unexplained, highly emotional drive that rises beyond reason. Modern critics suggest that Ferdinand has an incestuous fixation for his sister which accounts for his anger and frustration. Even if we cannot accept this overtly psychological explanation totally, it is inescapable that his feelings for his sister are such that he wishes her to remain a 'virtuous widow'. That wish has little to do with a concern for possessions or property. Neither are these feelings openly expressed to his brother, a Cardinal, happy with a mistress. They explode in anger and also impotence. The rage is accompanied by a paralysis of mind, frustrated from seeking reasonable retribution because his reasons cannot be publicly expressed. There is a growing tension composed of desire, guilt and anger which no action can satisfy or release. Apparent relief comes in the macabre tortures but, in fact, his mind turns from calculated madness to grotesque lycanthropy. The cord of reason is snapped by the sight of the dead Duchess. He makes fruitless excuses, attempts to blame Bosola, but his distraction is irreversible and he becomes a gibbering madman, compounding his error by stabbing his own brother. His hidden, destructive obsession, so disastrously nurtured, is exposed in his dying words: 'My sister! O! my sister! there's the cause on't'. (V.v. 71).

The Cardinal

At the opening of the play, Delio and Antonio present a very unflattering portrait of the Cardinal as a priest enjoying sensual pleasures, jealous, plotting in secret, working through spies, panders and professional villains. He typifies the Machiavellian antagonist, maintaining power through intrigue and deceit. There is a total absence of religious feelings. In keeping a mistress and becoming a soldier, the Cardinal is an entirely worldly, cruel churchman quick to poison or murder when a threat arises.

In outward appearance, however, the Cardinal presents a somewhat different figure, especially compared with his brother, the Duke. His language is less extreme, he counsels moderation at Ferdinand's jealous outburst, urging him to control himself. He takes no active part in the torture sequence. It is his relationship with Julia that precipitates his downfall. This affair, in which each party enjoys physical gratification, exposes a weakness in the Cardinal's otherwise impregnable armour. He treats the matter too carelessly. Though ready to discard Julia, he is seduced into revealing the truth about the Duchess's murder. He quickly realises his error, but it is too late. Faced with Julia's corpse, a maddened brother and a secretly antagonistic Bosola, the Cardinal's cool calculations fail. He, too, becomes a victim, slain by his own insane brother. Webster offers two contrasting verbal and visual images – the villain and the sober churchman. As the play progresses the two identities merge until at the climax he comes to represent the corrupt, unscrupulous manipulator that Antonio described at the outset.

Julia

Although her part is small, Julia plays a vital role in the display of corruption. She, too, is a victim of a corrupt society, moving restlessly from one lover to another, deceiving her husband, and paying a heavy price for her too-persistent questioning. Her prostitution of love sharply contrasts with the Duchess's passion for Antonio: one opportunistic, casual, deceptive; the other springing from mutual respect that encourages and endures.

Antonio

It is difficult to fix a firm personality on Antonio and critics vary in their estimate of his character. On the one hand he is portrayed as a loyal, virtuous servant, yet his actions are not those of a man with much courage or foresight. So far as sensibility is concerned, his stay in France has produced an admiration for 'fix'd order', a dislike of sycophants and a high regard for open and uncorrupt government. His assessment of the Duke and the Cardinal proves to be acutely correct. What he little suspects is that his admiration for the Duchess is reciprocated. The intensity of the Duchess's advance takes him by surprise. At first he makes bantering replies, but his hesitancy is overcome. Marriage to the Duchess, unthought of moments before, becomes a *fait accompli*. But the role required of him in such a secret marriage is outside his compass. He can play the husband but not the protector. He can never overcome his subservience as a steward. The Duchess makes all the decisions. He is embarrassed by the 'hat' incident in Act II, Scene i, when the Duchess tries to stress their equality. Bosola easily outwits him and he is quickly distracted by events surrounding the birth of the baby; 'I am lost in amazement. I know not what to think on't' (II.i. 173–4). Nothing in Antonio's previous experience helps him in this predicament. His behaviour combines naivety with rash, bungling attempts at deceit. The absence of immediate retribution lulls him into a false sense of security. While he is fully aware of the common condemnation of the Duchess he cannot devise means to check these imputations. His methods are clearly not in the machiavellian league. When their true relationship is inadvertently betrayed to Ferdinand, it is the quick-thinking Duchess who devises the escape plan. Whilst he may be an admirable servant and a loving husband, he lacks the qualities of a master. His naivety is again exposed in his belief that he can achieve reconciliation with the Duke and the Cardinal. Though it is unsuccessful, the attempt does reveal his personal bravery. Despite the admonition of Delio and the echoing, warning voice, he persists in his quest, only to receive a fatal wound and learn of his wife's death. Antonio's dying words, of 'bubbles blown in the air', show the fragility of his whole relationship with the Duchess. The delight he could enjoy, but the burden of responsibility is beyond his capacity and the bubble bursts. Honesty and virtue count for little in a corrupt, hostile world.

Cariola

Cariola also suffers in this inhospitable world. She quickly recognises the danger inherent in the Duchess's decision to marry Antonio, uncertain whether it is courage or foolhardiness. But she does stay with her mistress, keeping her secret, comforting her at the time of childbirth, delighting in the evident love between Antonio and the Duchess. She remains faithful during their adversity and suffers death like them. Only in the last few moments of her life does she struggle to escape. Her feigning pregnancy carries no weight, however, and she is strangled with the children – all innocent of any misdemeanour.

Minor characters

The bitter invective of the major characters is mirrored by the sycophantic courtiers. For example, the officers are quick to take their cue from Bosola in abusing Antonio. They intensify the feeling of a relentless, unjust parasitic society. Even the private, secret world that the Duchess would like to enjoy is invaded by a strange and miscellaneous mixture of 'extras'. Most unusual and frightening are the madmen whom the Duke uses to distract the Duchess. These extras provide a cross-section of society – lawyer, priest, doctor, tailor, farmer – all driven mad by the pressures and deceits of the world. We have the feeling of a society gone mad, where sanity, integrity and love cannot survive. The two pilgrims at the Shrine lament this state of affairs. Commenting on Antonio's banishment they draw a general conclusion 'All things do help th' unhappy man to fall'. The world conspires to destroy rather than uplift the fallen.

10.3 STYLE

The comments on Webster's borrowings in *The White Devil* are equally applicable to *The Duchess of Malfi*. J. R. Brown, in *The Revels* text, provides an appendix listing at least twenty authors from whom Webster has borrowed literary ideas, incidents, allusions, references or pieces of the story. All are carefully footnoted. Nevertheless, the overall style of the play does not represent a miscellaneous combination of twenty different writers. Again Webster manages to transform his borrowings, perhaps by the alteration of a few words, a change of emphasis or the strengthening of an image so that the text is neither disjointed nor rough, but flowing and continuous.

The particular style that Webster has created may be identified by comparing it with a dew-dappled cobweb viewed against a dark background. The world of *The Duchess of Malfi* becomes increasingly sombre as it moves into the prison and murder scenes. Many of the earlier episodes also take place at night. But the language of the play, strong, economical and delicate, stretches over this darkness with a sharp, poetic brilliance. The 'dew' diamonds highlight particular junctions in the web with images drawn from many sources, yet dramatically apposite to the atmosphere of the play. The Duchess's courtship of Antonio is physically focused on a shining gold ring. It is the cure for bloodshot eyes and the hiding-place for a 'saucy and ambitious devil', displaced when the ring is eased onto his finger. In their love-tryst, the story of Paris and the golden apples illuminates Antonio's admiring words. Later the Duchess speaks of a dream:

> Methought I wore my coronet of state,
> And on a sudden all the diamonds
> were changed to pearls (III.v. 13-15).

Antonio replies:

> My interpretation
> Is, you'll weep shortly, for to me
> The pearls do signify your tears (III.v. 15-17).

Here imagery and actuality correspond. Diamonds become misted pearls. Joy becomes sorrow. Even in the dark horror of the prison, Bosola urges the Duchess 'Look you, the stars shine still' (IV.i. 99). This image pierces the gloom. Diamonds and pearls reappear at the moment the Duchess is being strangled. She declares:

> What would it pleasure me to have my throat cut
> With diamonds?. . . or to be shot to death with pearls?
> (IV.ii. 216-18).

These unexpected, vivid metaphors introduce a cold brilliance to the macabre reality. The obsession with death and decay is redeemed by the poetry.

Language and character

An obvious example is Bosola whose language is coarse, full of sexual puns and innuendoes, deriding moral qualities of honour or honesty, quick to adopt a style less bawdy but still sardonic when talking to the Duke and the Cardinal. Later a change in style hints at, but does not confirm, an altered attitude in his recommendation of Antonio's good qualities. His soft words are sufficient to persuade her to trust him with her secrets. A real transformation occurs in the murder scene when Bosola's speeches are freed from bawdiness and reveal depths of feeling and an awareness of compassion and pity not previously sensed. It is through the style of his language that Webster informs us of this new mood. Changed feelings are made explicit in language but their practical effect is nullified by the carnage of the final sequence.

Early in the play it is the Duke's language rather than his actions that informs us of his character. His edginess and uncertain temper is shown in the abruptness of his reprimands to his courtiers. The wildness that breaks the surface when he hears of the marriage is expressed in fierce images drawn from drugs and purging - mandrake, rhubarb, pitch, fire, sulphur, cupping - as if the Duchess had suffered some terrible disease. This excessive, denunciatory language seems to warn of a mind tortured and obsessed. In his demented lycanthropic state, the distraction is uncontrolled; words pour out in disconnected, rambling assertions as his reason breaks down. The profuseness of the Duke contrasts with the terse, restrained, controlled style of the Cardinal. Except on two fatal occasions, his mask stays put. Though often severe, he can tease and wheedle as Julia finds to her cost. He is a little too clever in protecting his mad brother. Logic and lucidity cannot protect him from destruction. In the increasingly desperate cries for help, the control breaks down and the mask cracks. His only escape seems to lie in oblivion:

> . Let me
> Be laid by, and never thought of. (V.v. 89-90)

> A strange epitaph for the powerful soldier-cleric.

The language that the Duchess uses enhances her personality. As occasion demands, she can be fierce and spirited in debate with her brothers, sensual and feminine with Antonio, courageous and unbowed in the physical ordeal with the lunatics and listening to Bosola's nerve-breaking homily as the Executioner. When the brothers pressure her about remarriage she retorts:

> Diamonds are of most value
> They say, that have pass'd through most jewellers' hands
> (I.i. 299-300)

For Antonio she voices an encouraging, stimulating invitation:

> This is flesh and blood, sir:
> 'Tis not the figure cut in alabaster
> Kneels at my husband's tomb. (I.i. 453-55).

Close to death, she kneels proudly, yet patiently:

> heaven-gates are not so highly arch'd
> As princes' palaces, they that enter there
> Must go upon their knees (IV.ii. 232-4).

The style, tone and imagery of the character's words combine to create a subtle, individual voice.

Couplets that complete a scene or mark a character's departure often act as a moral comment on the events that have just taken place. For example, having discovered the dropped horoscope, Bosola declares:

> Though lust do mask in ne'er so strange disguise
> She's oft found witty, but is never wise (II.iii. 76-7).

There is an ironic truth in Bosola's insinuating remarks. Such comments are also expanded in slightly longer fables. The Duchess tells the story of the salmon and the dog-fish (III.v. 125–41) ending it with the moral 'Men oft are valued high, when th'are most wretched'. These shorter and longer literary interjections combine to suggest or imply rather than state a moral perspective. Their effect is often ironic, emphasising the absence of honesty, truth or fidelity rather than any conventional moralising.

Use of irony and humour

Part of the complexity of Bosola's character is created by his skilful use of irony and humour that invests the whole play with a certain grim amusement. His jokes, observations and asides savour of what today is called 'black' humour. He finds in the solemn or macabre an opportunity to mock seriousness or joke about horror. He is described as the 'court-gall', one who torments, rails, disparages often through a pun or aphorism. His own imprisonment is described with a sarcastic humour: 'Black-birds fatten best in hard weather' (I.i. 37). He is fond of parasitic images – crows, magpies, caterpillars, leeches, all feeding off the rotten or the dead. Time and time again he takes ideas from medicine or physics or witchcraft using the references to disparage human aspirations. There is an abrasive brilliance in his derogatory remarks: for example, a face cream made of 'fat of serpents, spawn of snakes, Jews' spittle and their young children's ordure' (II.i. 35–6). He actually presents apricots ripened in horse-dung to the Duchess, omitting to tell her until after she has eaten them.

These humorous, gross comments full of political jest or sexual innuendo not only create the character of Bosola. Explicit evidence in the play of deceit, treachery, cruelty corroborates much that Bosola decries. The ring of truth is heard in his black ironic humour.

10.4 STAGECRAFT

Whilst there is talk of specific locations – Malfi, Rome, Ancona – these places do not have much geographical significance. We are never concerned with the citizens of Malfi nor how far it is from Malfi to Ancona. Webster has an entirely different purpose in locating the action of the play as he does. The notes on structure discussed the division of the play into five acts – Court, Bedchamber, World, Prison, Grave – locations that are symbolic rather than specific. They give opportunity for vividly contrasting stage pictures. The opening scene presents a bustle of courtiers, whispered consultations and the luxury of a Court with the Duke surrounded by syco-phantic followers. The Bedchamber is intimate, private, with the vain ceremony of the Court displaced by a display of genuine, deeply-felt love. The World scene is full of action – angry exits, arrival of guards, accusatory charges and arrests. The loving intimacy of the bedroom gives way to horrible exposure before the world.

Half-way through the play, Webster begins a major shift in the style of presentation from the realistic to the symbolic. First we see the ceremonial mime in Act III. The episode at Ancona before the shrine of Our Lady of Loretto shows the Cardinal symbolically discarding his religious vestments and assuming the armour of a soldier. Now he represents martial law and the first to experience its power are Antonio and the Duchess. They are banished and the wedding-ring torn from the Duchess's finger. The triumphant ceremony of the instalment with the solemn music and chanting offers a striking visual contrast to the pettiness of the banishment. The demonstrated power of the State is visited upon the head of the unfortunate Duchess.

In the Prison sequence we witness a grisly ritual. The tableau of waxen figures and the parade of madmen is followed by the ritual of torture and slaughter concluding with the Duchess's own death. Her demise introduces the Grave sequence. One by one the living become corpses – victims of strangling, poisoning, and stabbing. In the stage picture of the opening scene, the Duke and Cardinal demonstrated their power and utter self-confidence. Now one is a grovelling, mad wolf-man and the other desperately plotting to avoid exposure. The corpse-strewn stage seen at the play's end represents a horrifying *memento mori* tableau. Death overtakes all – good and bad.

By gradually changing the style of presentation from the realistic to the stylised, Webster lifts the events above the reality from which they were derived to a higher symbolic level so that the play becomes a universal model of human frailty, obsession and destruction and not merely the retelling of a bloodthirsty Italian horror-story.

Not only do we hear the language of violence and love, but we witness its effect on stage. For example, the turbulent Duke seems to offer a physical threat in his admonition to the Duchess with the offer of the dagger. She uses a ring to soothe Antonio's bloodshot eye as a prelude to courtship. There is a constant physical energy in touching, kneeling, kissing, the devouring of apricots, the dropping of the horoscope. As the play moves to its climax this action becomes wilder, more unbridled. The ferocity of the language is matched by the horrors of poisoning and stabbing. Even the relatively quiet passage when Antonio moves towards the Cardinal's palace is disturbed by a ghostly echo. Every action underlines the continuing, inescapable danger in which the Duchess and Antonio find themselves. The relentlessness of the revenge is reinforced by a series of stage-pictures, sometimes realistic, sometimes symbolic. Webster uses his mastery of stagecraft to present a variety of shifting theatrical impressions that continually engage us. As the play proceeds, the symbolic tends to supersede the realistic and the final Act needs to be viewed in terms of ritualistic retribution rather than a last-ditch shoot-out.

11 SPECIMEN PASSAGE AND COMMENTARY

THE DUCHESS OF MALFI

Act II, Scene ii

Enter BOSOLA

BOSOLA So, so: there's no question but her tetchiness and most vulturous eating of the apricots are apparent signs of breeding

Enter Old Lady

Now?

OLD LADY I am in haste, sir.

BOSOLA There was a young waiting-woman had a monstrous desire to see the glass-house.

OLD LADY Nay, pray let me go:-

BOSOLA And it was only to know what strange instrument it was should swell up a glass to the fashion of a woman's belly.

OLD LADY I will hear no more of the glass-house – you are still abusing women!

BOSOLA Who I? no, only (by the way now and then) mention your frailties. The orange tree bears ripe and green fruit, and blossoms all together: and some of you give entertainment for pure love: but more, for precious reward. The lusty spring smells well: but drooping autumn tastes well: if we have the same golden showers that rained in the time of Jupiter the Thunderer, you have the same Danäes still, to hold up their laps to receive them:- didst thou never study the mathematics?

OLD LADY What's that, sir?

BOSOLA Why, to know the trick to make many lines meet in one centre:- go, go; give your foster-daughters good counsel: tell them that the devil takes delight to hang at a woman's girdle,

like a false rusty watch, that she cannot discern how the time
passes.

Exit Old Lady

Enter ANTONIO, DELIO, RODERIGO, GRISOLAN

ANTONIO Shut up the court gates:-

RODERIGO   Why sir? what's the danger?

ANTONIO Shut up the posterns presently: and call
      All the officers o' the' court.

GRISOLAN I shall instantly

Exit

ANTONIO Who keeps the key o' the' park gate?

RODERIGO   Forobosco.

ANTONIO Let him bring 't presently.

Enter GRISOLAN *with Officers*

1st Officer O, gentlemen o' th' court, the foulest treason!

BOSOLA (*aside*) If that these apricocks should be poison'd now,
      Without my knowledge!

1st Officer There was taken even now a Switzer in the duchess'
      bedchamber.

2nd Officer A Switzer?

1st Officer With a pistol in his great cod-piece.

BOSOLA Ha, ha, ha!

1st Officer The cod-piece was the case for't.

2nd Officer There was a cunning traitor. Who would have searched
      his cod-piece?

1st Officer True, if he had kept out of the ladies' chambers:- and
      all the moulds of his buttons were leaden bullets.

2nd Officer O, wicked cannibal! a fire-lock in's cod-piece!

1st Officer 'Twas a French plot, upon my life.

2nd Officer To see what the devil can do!

ANTONIO All the officers here?

Officers We are:-

ANTONIO Gentlemen,
      We have lost much plate you know; and but this evening
      Jewels, to the value of four thousand ducats
      Are missing in the duchess' cabinet –
      Are the gates shut?

Officers Yes.

ANTONIO   'Tis the duchess' pleasure
      Each officer be lock'd into his chamber
      Till the sun-rising: and to send the keys
      Of all their chests, and their outward doors,
      Into her bedchamber:- she is very sick.

RODERIGO At her pleasure.
ANTONIO She entreats you take't not ill: the innocent
    Shall be the more approv'd by it.
BOSOLA Gentleman o' the' wood-yard, where's your Switzer now?
1st Officer By this hand, 'twas credibly reported by one o' the black
    guard.

                            Exeunt all except ANTONIO *and* DELIO
DELIO How fares it with the duchess?
ANTONIO   She's expos'd
    Unto the worst of torture, pain and fear:-
DELIO Speak to her all happy comfort.
ANTONIO How do I play the fool with mine own dagger!
    You are this night, dear friend, to post to Rome:
    My life lies in your service.
DELIO Do not doubt me –
ANTONIO O, 'tis far from me: and yet fear presents me
    Somewhat that looks like danger.
DELIO   Believe it,
    'Tis but the shadow of your fear, no more:
    How superstitiously we mind our evils!
    The throwing down salt, or crossing of a hare,
    Bleeding at nose, the stumbling of a horse,
    Or singing of a cricket, are of pow'r
    To daunt whole man in us. Sir, fare you well:
    I wish you all the joys of a bless'd father;
    And, for my faith, lay this unto your breast –
    Old friends, like old swords, still are trusted best.

                                      Exit
                                 Enter CARIOLA
CARIOLA Sir, you are the happy father of a son –
    Your wife commends him to you.
ANTONIO   Blessed comfort:
    For heaven-sake tend her well; I'll presently
    Go set a figure for's nativity.

                                 Exeunt

    The scene as a whole falls into four parts: Bosola's exchange with the midwife, the excitement of the alleged theft, the intimate conversation between Antonio and Delio and the concluding announcement of the birth. Webster treats each of these sections in a distinctive style. The first part, in prose, typifies the language of the bawdy, suspicous Bosola. He coarsely refers to the Duchess's tetchiness and 'vulturous' eating. The conversation with the midwife hints at sexual misconduct. He successfully debases the delicate imagery drawn from the orange tree which bears ripe and green fruit and blossom all at once by comparing young women's love-making ('lusty spring') with older women's profit from the practice ('drooping autumn tastes well'). His next image is taken from Greek mythology when a shower of gold enabled Jupiter to seduce Danäe. Bosola crudely reduces this story to an observation that women are still persuaded by money. He converts the maxim 'Many ways meet in one town' into 'Many lines meet in one centre' giving the saying a sexual *double entendre*. Women enjoy intimacies, heedless of time, encouraged by the devil hanging at their girdle like a 'false rusty watch'. The effect of this opening section is to devalue love into lust in crude images juxtaposed with delicate, classical references.

With the arrival of Antonio and the officers, the tone changes. The language becomes direct and unambiguous, though Bosola continues his crudities with jokes about codpieces and pistols. In these mocking observations we are given clear insights into Bosola's canny intelligence as well as his pungent, critical and crude humour. His joking manner reveals disbelief in Antonio's subterfuges to preserve secrecy. In his mocking asides, he shows no inclination to search for the alleged thieves, but he makes no direct challenge to Antonio concerning the true purpose of the deception. He keeps his own counsel, letting his guard slip only once with the remarks about the possibility of poisoned apricots.

Although Antonio appears calm and controlled with the officers, his apprehension soon shows through when he is left alone with Delio. Perhaps Bosola's attitude has affected him. Words like 'torture', 'pain' and 'fear' are used to highlight the danger of the Duchess's position and, for himself, Antonio fears that he has 'played the fool' with his own dagger – taken too many risks. This conversation clearly reveals Antonio's worry about the dangers that may threaten their security. Delio tries to alleviate this uneasiness with a series of homely superstitions about impending disasters that should be laughed off: spilling the salt, a stumbling horse – folk images that Webster has borrowed from other writers. Delio's light-hearted recitation suggests that they can be disregarded. But one in his list, 'bleeding of the nose', we are to see enacted in the next scene and the event troubles Antonio greatly.

Delio's exit is marked with a *sententia*. Webster reworks the old proverb 'Old friends and old wine are best' to 'Old friends, like old swords, still are trusted best'. The warmth of 'old wine' is replaced by the harder image of 'old swords' and the introduction of 'trusted' intensifies the need for loyalty in these particular circumstances.

In the final section, Webster chooses to treat the actual cause of all the consternation with extreme brevity in Cariola's two-line speech. Antonio, now a happy father and a loved husband, is momentarily content. We notice that whilst Delio scoffed at portents, Antonio is anxious to gain knowledge of the future from the calculation of the new baby's horoscope. This intention, contained within a rhyming couplet, formally completes the scene.

Although the episode is only eighty-five lines in length, it is crammed with action, varied in pace and style. The plot is moved significantly forward with the birth of the baby and the consequences that ensue. The prose exchange between Bosola and the midwife consists principally of a leisurely harangue against women. Then the stage is suddenly filled and the pace quickened with the arrival of Antonio and the officers. The bawdiness persists, but is eventually replaced with more serious instruction for search and confinement. Antonio's private fears are revealed in his conversation with Delio, though the tension is reduced by his friend's light-hearted riposte. The climax of the scene comes abruptly with Cariola's brief announcement. This could easily have concluded the scene, but Webster advances the plot in the final line by initiating a complication to be explored in the following scene.

The scene illustrates the wide-ranging diversity and vividness of Webster's dramatic style in prose and verse. Details of importance are added to the characters of the two stewards. Bosola becomes increasingly brash and suspicious, though he has yet to discover that Antonio has married the Duchess. Antonio's hurriedly devised excuses carry little conviction and with the departure of Delio, he becomes even more isolated. The battle between the two men gathers intensity, and bitterness develops in the scene that follows as a logical development.

PART III: CRITICAL RECEPTION

12 CRITICAL RECEPTION

12.1 THE PLAYS IN PERFORMANCE

Webster expressed his own dissatisfaction with the first performance of *The White Devil*. Whilst approving of the acting he wrote 'it was acted, in so dull a time of winter, presented in so open and black a theatre, that it wanted (that which is the only grace and setting out of a tragedy) a full and understanding auditory'. (To the Reader, *The White Devil*, Revels edn, p.2). However repeat performances and a production of *The Duchess of Malfi* at the Blackfriars Theatre were much more popular. When they appeared in print, the plays went through several editions.

Restoration audiences also enjoyed the plays with famous actors like Thomas Betterton gaining great applause for his interpretations of the principal roles. Later, in the eighteenth century, the texts began to undergo what were considered 'improving' revisions. *The White Devil* was revised by Nahum Tate (who had also carried out a revision of Shakespeare's *King Lear*) and the play retitled *Injured Love* or *The Cruel Husband* (1707). Lewis Theobold offered *The Duchess of Malfi* in a new guise, entitled *The Fatal Secret* (1735). The intention of these editors was to remove the 'errors' from Webster's writing, tidy up the plots and clarify characters and their motivations. Theobald commented on the author's 'wide and undigested genius', his eccentricity and his lack of clarity. Webster had failed to observe the rules of dramatic construction. In reality, these revisions knocked the heart out of the plays making them conventional in style and mechanical in construction.

Closer to this century, a famous theatre-director, William Poel, started the Elizabethan Stage Society with a view to presenting plays of that period in a style close to the original. The scenery was kept basic and great attention was paid to speaking the verse effectively. The action of the plays was made continuous without the usual breaks for intervals. In 1892, William Poel produced *The Duchess of Malfi*. The audience included the well known critic and poet, A. C. Swinburne who wrote of his pleasure 'in seeing that transcendent masterpiece of tragedy restored to the stage under such favourable circumstances'. The theatre critic William Archer was much less impressed. His article in *The New Review* published in the following year was a response to the performance which he condemned in wholesale terms. He could find little to admire in the plot, the characters or their motivations.

In 1945 a production of *The Duchess of Malfi* was mounted by John Gielgud and Peggy Ashcroft in association with a Cambridge don, George Rylands. A critic, Edmund Wilson, wrote of this presentation 'You might have thought that Webster's style was too precious for the stage, but every speech has its force and point'. The anonymous critic of *The Times* also found much to praise in the production. Skilled acting combined with imaginative direction succeeded in giving theatrical life to Webster's play, proving its effectiveness in performance.

The cover of the programme for the National Theatre's production of *The White Devil* in 1969 showed spiders spinning gilded webs. The characters in the play were costumed rather like brilliant insects: moths, butterflies, spiders. Head-dresses, collars and ruffs looked like transparent wings. Bodies were tightly cased in shiny black bodices or trunks. Rupert Brooke's comment about the 'writhing grubs' was the inspiration for these designs. One critic commented on 'Webster's gaudy monsters of the play who come to life in a recognisable whole'.

Frank Dunlop, who directed the production, contributed a programme note:

> It is not just a flashy, conventional Italianate tragedy of revenge. It is a machiavellian political intrigue and a devastating intimate study of the nastier side of man... For every action there seems to be an observer. We see things not only through our own eyes but also through the eyes of some witness in the play. It is as though Webster is determined that we must be made to think more deeply by observing the same actions and thoughts in infinite variations and see beyond what we often take as truth... Webster may be obsessed with the despair of living but the grandeur of defiance of his characters for the horrors of the world and the means he uses to express it are a joy. (*Programme Note*, National Theatre, 1969.)

In the 1985 production of *The Duchess of Malfi* at the National Theatre, the director (Philip Prowse) was also the designer. He was able to give special attention to staging the spectacular theatrical ceremonies and processions in which Webster delighted. The courtly costumes were in sombre black and greys illuminated by shafts of light that cut through the surrounding darkness. One critic, Robert Hewison, found that the production emphasised 'blood and lust, indeed lust after someone of one's own blood' (*Sunday Times*, July 1985). However it tended to undervalue the political facets of the play so that Bosola's devious dealings with his employer and secret paymasters received insufficient emphasis. The strength of the presentation lay 'in the transubstantiation of blood and lust into death'. Such a view of the governing idea of the play does much to commend *The Duchess of Malfi* as a classical Jacobean tragedy.

12.2 CRITICISM

Whatever your views on Webster, you will find that they are contradicted or echoed by the critics. Controversy about the quality of Webster's dramatic output has continued to rage since the plays were first written. Before the present century, the enthusiasts for his work were particularly impressed by his poetic skills. Charles Lamb praised his 'intenseness of feeling', Swinburne admired the way 'his passionate and daring genius attains the utmost limit and rounds the final goal of tragedy: never once does it break the bounds of poetic instinct'. (G. K. Hunter and S. K. Hunter (eds), *John Webster: A Critical Anthology* (Harmondsworth, 1969) p. 68). These views were condemned out of hand by the nineteenth-century theatre critic William Archer as 'extravagant and wanton paradoxes'. He was particularly damning about the weak dramatic structure of the plays, loosely put together and implausibly motivated. Archer admitted that Webster might be a great poet, but as a playwright he 'wrote haphazard dramatic and melodramatic romances for an eagerly receptive but semi-barbarous public , (Hunter and Hunter, 1969, p.68) or as Charles Kingsley put it: 'he wrote "for effect not truth" '. More recently, the poet Rupert Brooke referred to Webster's plays as 'full of the feverish and ghostly turmoil of a nest of maggots'.

It is probably useful to examine the contentious issues separately: his literary skill, the form and devices of theatre, and questions of morality. A strange paradox emerges when assessing Webster's poetic skills. Whilst there is widespread agreement that a substantial proportion of his literary references represented 'borrowings' from other authors, this purloined poetry gains considerable admiration. Though Webster's works may be strongly derivative, in no sense do they resemble other authors' plays. John Russell Brown comments: 'Webster did not borrow with a quiescent mind; rather, imitation quickened his own invention'. He does not devalue the quotations but enhances them. We can admire Webster for this particular and peculiar skill that absorbs, rephrases, restresses, even reversing meanings, allusions or expressions of feeling.

Critics admire Webster's use of his poetic skill, not for decorative embroidery, but to illuminate particular themes and the characters who embody them. For example, Hereward Price identifies the 'relentless repetition' of images of corruption, poison, infection and the devil. Not only are they present in figurative language, but also in the characters and their actions. Vittoria *is* a 'white devil'. Isabella, Bracciano and Julia *are* actually poisoned. The Duke *is* infected by madness. Of the playwright's imagery, Price says: 'It is the most pregnant expression of truth. It reveals character, it does the work of argument, it emphasises mood, and it prefigures the events to come' (Hunter and Hunter, 1969, p.179). Gabriele Baldini reinforces this notion of double purpose when noting that the stage picture also illuminates motives and feelings. He cites particularly the ravings of the poisoned, maddened Bracciano and the eccentric behaviour of the demented Duke. Bracciano's brain has been 'on fire' throughout the play in the excess of his sensual desire for Vittoria. The poisoned helmet physically exposes that passion. The controlled obsession of the Duke is given terrifying release in his lycanthropic lunging at shadows. In other words, the imagery reinforces the actions and reveals the reality of the characters' inner feelings (Hunter and Hunter, 1969, p.164).

Clifford Leech comments particularly on the use of fables and *sententiae*, observing that these literary devices arising from a specific moment in the play also take on a generalised meaning. They offer an objective comment on the events, ideas and themes contained in the plays. The general consensus of these critics is that Webster's poetic skills are integral to the play, the characters and their feelings. This poetic technique is subtle, conscious and well planned. Despite the diversity of sources from which they are drawn, the images acquire a special dramatic coherence that is unique to Webster (Hunter and Hunter, 1969, p.268).

Archer's denunciation of Webster's rambling, loose, disconnected, unrealistic structure has been countered by a number of commentators who have explored the problems associated with convention and realism. In writing his plays, Webster was no doubt aware of the tastes of the sophisticated, yet violence-loving, Jacobean audience and of the particular melodramatic theatrical forms that had popular appeal. Numerous contemporary plays were stuffed with physically horrific acts, murders, poisoning, bloodshed, madness, ghosts, spectres.

It has been observed by some commentators that there is a logic in Webster's plays which, while not conforming to Archer's notion of the well-made play, still has a certain validity when contemporary Jacobean conventions are recognised. For example, J. Smith points out in a careful analysis of the speeches in *The White Devil* that apparently inconsequential chatter between the characters succeeds in evoking an evil, amoral, self-seeking, revengeful world and predicts only too clearly what is going to happen in the play (Hunter and Hunter, 1969, pp.114 ff). A society in which ordered thought should predominate is distorted by passion, grudge, greed and jealousy. Bloodthirsty events in the play do not simply pander to popular cravings, but symbolise the absence of moral or spiritual values. Professor Muriel Bradbrook notes that the opposition of Fate and Chance intrigued the Jacobeans and that reference in the plays to witchcraft, horoscopes, omens and dreams reflects this concern (Hunter and Hunter, 1969, p.161). Cecil comments that the ghosts and tortures are symbolic representations of spiritual terror and diabolical delight in suffering. This treatment gives a dimension of true tragedy to otherwise repulsive events. Inga-Stina Ekeblad, investigating the masque of madmen, clearly reveals its derivation from a particular form of masque that mocked remarried widows for their luxurious flouting of convention (Hunter and Hunter, 1969, p.202). The trial of the Duchess becomes a funeral masque. The 'wedding' gifts to the widow are a coffin, cord and funeral bell. Reexamination of the proposal scene between the Duchess and Antonio reveals the emphasis on 'wills', 'winding sheets', '*Quietus est*' - objects and sayings associated with death. So the betrothal scene and the death scene are symbolically linked, both ceremonial and ritualised. Calderwood stresses the regular occurrence of ceremony and ritual through the plays. Appearance is often contained in public ceremonial whilst reality is expressed in private scenes. So the whole pattern of the events in the plays is drawn from ritual, symbolic, ceremonial and mimetic styles of drama that together create a vivid and coherent picture, rather like a mosaic of a world in which danger, threat and discord lurk beneath ordered, controlled appearance. This form of drama, though drawing on numerous conventions, may come to represent the reality of distress and chaos more effectively than the logic of a well-made play. Webster's plays stress the *illogic* of human passion and greed where motives are often submerged, half-understood or suppressed.

Perhaps the greatest debate lies in judgements on the morality, immorality or amorality of Webster's plays. Peter Murray writes:

> Webster shows that the worldly life of courts and courtiers is vain, and that integrity cannot finally defeat such evil, but there is another kind of life possible, a life deriving its values from moments of love and sharing and mercy that may create happiness on earth, for however brief a time, and hope for a life hereafter that will last eternally (Holdsworth, 1984, p.179).

He sees the suffering of the Duchess of Malfi relating to the suffering of Job. Lord David Cecil sees Webster 'as a stern moral teacher whose plays are carefully designed to enforce the philosophy of human conduct in which he believes' (Hunter and Hunter, 1979, p.154). He claims that the couplets which conclude the plays:

> Let guilty men remember their black deeds
> Do lean on crutches made of slender reeds.

and

> Integrity of life is fame's best friend
> Which nobly, beyond death, shall crown the end

are true summaries of the plays' intentions which explore the consequence of sin and the process of repentance. The confrontations portrayed on the stage symbolise spiritual battles.

The firmest opposition to a moralistic reading is found in Ian Jack's criticism. He is of the view that the plays lack 'a profound and *balanced* insight into life' (Holdsworth, 1984, p.76). He does not believe that there is any real correspondence between the pious axioms and the life represented in the drama. Disorder, decadence, machiavellian anarchy is the order of the day and Webster indulges in presenting fantastic extravaganzas of horror. George Bernard Shaw christened Webster 'the Tussaud laureate', suggesting that the plays were animated versions of Madame Tussaud's Chamber of Horrors. Modern society's experience of horrific warfare, gang violence, mass starvation, rioting and political assassination has removed the sense of remoteness and inexplicability of such actions. They come close to our painful sense of reality, regularly confronted with mindless killing, terrorism and death. Positive moral values seem to make little headway in contemporary society against a tide of aggression and excessive materialism. This negative charge does not however completely overcome a dogged positive concern for unselfish compassion. The imbalance in Webster's plays might find a realistic echo in the tenuous grip on order and morality exhibited in the modern world.

REVISION QUESTIONS

1. 'Tussaud laureate.' G. B. Shaw equates Webster's plays with the Waxwork Chamber of Horrors devised by Madame Tussaud. How far do you agree with this assessment of Webster as a playwright?
2. 'A stern moral teacher.' What in *The White Devil* supports this view of Webster as a playwright?
3. How successfully does Webster match language and character in *The Duchess of Malfi*?
4. To what extent does Vittoria engage our sympathies as 'a white devil'?
5. Compare and contrast the characters of Bosola and Flamineo.
6. Discuss the balance of reality and theatricality in *The White Devil*.
7. Which characters in *The Duchess of Malfi* demonstrate machiavellian motives?
8. Comment on the effectiveness of Webster's 'borrowing' in either *The White Devil* or *The Duchess of Malfi*.
9. 'A great poet but not a great dramatist.' Discuss this view of Webster with reference to either *The White Devil* or *The Duchess of Malfi*.

FURTHER READING

Texts

The White Devil
Brown, John Russell (ed.) *The White Devil* (Methuen, 1960).
Brennan, Elizabeth M. (ed.) *The White Devil* (Benn, 1966).

The Duchess of Malfi
Brown, John Russell (ed.) *The Duchess of Malfi* (Methuen, 1964).
Brennan, Elizabeth M. (ed.) *The Duchess of Malfi* (Benn, 1964).

Commentary

Bowers, F. T., *Elizabethan Revenge Tragedy* (Cambridge University Press, 1940).
Bradbrook, M. C., *Themes and Conventions of Elizabethan Tragedy* (Cambridge University Press, 1935); *John Webster: Citizen and Dramatist* (Weidenfeld and Nicolson, 1980).
Eliot, T. S., *Selected Essays* (Faber, 1931).
Ellis-Fermor, U., *Jacobean Drama* (Methuen, 1958) 4th edn.
Heinemann, M., *Puritanism and Theatre* (Cambridge University Press, 1980).
Holdsworth, R. V. (ed.) *Webster: The White Devil and The Duchess of Malfi* (Macmillan, 1984) rev. edn.
Hunter, G. K. and Hunter, S. K. (eds) *John Webster: Penguin Critical Anthology* (Harmondsworth, 1969).
Leech, C. and Craik, T. W. (eds) *The Revels History of Drama in English* (Methuen, 1975) vol. III.
Leech, C., *Webster; A Critical Study* (Arnold, 1951).
Lever, J. W., *Tragedy of State* (Methuen, 1971).
Morris, B., *John Webster: Mermaid Critical Commentaries* (Benn, 1970).
Mulryne, J. R., 'The Duchess of Malfi' in *Jacobean Theatre: Stratford-upon-Avon Studies* (Arnold, 1960) vol. I.

Ornstein, R., *The Moral Vision of Jacobean Tragedy* (Madison, 1960).
Rabkin, N., *Twentieth Century Interpretations of 'The Duchess of Malfi'* (New Jersey, 1968).

Mastering English Literature
Richard Gill

Mastering English Literature will help readers both to enjoy English Literature and to be successful in 'O' levels, 'A' levels and other public exams. It is an introduction to the study of poetry, novels and drama which helps the reader in four ways - by providing ways of approaching literature, by giving examples and practice exercises, by offering hints on how to write about literature, and by the author's own evident enthusiasm for the subject. With extracts from more than 200 texts, this is an enjoyable account of how to get the maximum satisfaction out of reading, whether it be for formal examinations or simply for pleasure.

Work Out English Literature ('A' level)
S.H. Burton

This book familiarises 'A' level English Literature candidates with every kind of test which they are likely to encounter. Suggested answers are worked out step by step and accompanied by full author's commentary. The book helps students to clarify their aims and establish techniques and standards so that they can make appropriate responses to similar questions when the examination pressures are on. It opens up fresh ways of looking at the full range of set texts, authors and critical judgements and motivates students to know more of these matters.

Also published by Macmillan

Mastering English Language S. H. Burton
Mastering English Grammar S. H. Burton
Workout English Language ('O' level and GCSE) S. H. Burton